跨文化能力：学习与实训

于群 编著

翻译：杨芸 王欣
顾问：Jan Van Maele
校对：Julia Hofmann
摄影/插画：于群

 南京大学出版社

Passing Through Your Intercultural Tunnel

Yu Qun

Translation: Yang Yun   Wang Xin
Consultant: Jan Van Maele
Proof reading: Julia Hofmann
Photography/illustration: Yu Qun

致读者

一、理想、信任和努力

全球化的进程使当今人们的流动性大大增加,大家不经意间就接触到了很多其它的语言、文化习俗和文化观念,进入各种"他文化"或文化混搭的情境中。

有句俗话,叫做"知易行难"。很多人对"跨文化能力"(intercultural competence)这个概念并不陌生,也有一定的跨文化经历,但生活在不同文化环境中仍然遭遇焦虑、不适和矛盾。其原因可能是大家在跨文化交流过程中没有接触和掌握一些应对技能和策略,**也不相信在很大程度上人们有意愿、有能力可以一起舒适地、创造性地解决矛盾和不适**。在全球范围内,文化观念差异和身份认同差异所导致的排他、仇恨情绪,更是产生各种冲突乃至战争的原因之一。

本书聚焦于相异甚至相悖的文化观念引发的、比较激烈的一些跨文化冲突形式,如争执、焦虑、冲撞等,**从相信人们可以出于善意(good will)而真诚互动**的根本点出发,从帮助处于跨文化冲突中的**某个个体**走出**焦虑和窘境**的根本考虑出发,从"知和行"两个方面同时介入,既简要地介绍相关理论,又紧密扣住"个体实际需求和操作步骤"来设置单元结构和内容,希望能够帮助大家在概括性地理解"跨文化能力"基本内涵的同时,又掌握一些相关技能,真正地操作运用,并受益其中,在各种"跨文化通道"中获得某种"自在"的感受。

虽然很多时候跨文化交流的过程不需要"出卖灵魂"或从"底线"让步,但最深刻、最能撬动沟通的跨文化对话,仍然是文化观念上的对话。然而,让人们在争执中松动原来坚定的文化观念,和其它相异甚至相悖的文化观念发生互动,是非常困难的事情,需要人们付出极大的努力,因为人们的自我认同正是基于这些坚定的观念甚至信仰。正如Dean Rickles 在为著名的物理学家 Bohm 晚年的著作《论对话》(*On Dialogue*)(2014)写的前言中所说:"**玻姆式对话需要努力——它是一个积极进取的过程,它需要类似于佛教所说的某种程度的自我否认,也需要在某种程度上对本我的消灭。**"

一些读者可能认为,跨文化能力构成与价值观念、身份认同、权利较量等概念有着密不可分的联系;同时,某个个体的跨文化调适过程其实很大程度上受到当时情境下其心理和性格因素的影响。因此,把"移情""尊重""延迟判断"等作为重要的跨文化技巧去倡导,可能过于简单化和理想化,或者老生常谈,并不能帮助直接形成全面的跨文化

"动态调整"的能力。但编写者仍然认为,**这些"理想化"的能力对于一个个体在一个具体的跨文化情境中,是非常必要和基础的**,即使受限于各种外部权力、要求或自身性格、交际动机,他不能够一味地去做到开放、尊重、移情和对话,这些仍然是**值得时时考虑、处处尝试和争取的**。

二、编写主题和思路

本书主要探讨以下一些问题:

》怎样理解文化?什么是跨文化能力?
》跨文化能力训练中有哪些是比较关键和实用的步骤?我怎样理解和操作?
》跨文化能力的衡量如何可能?

本书编写学理主要有以下几点:

(1) 本书统一使用"intercultural competence"(跨文化能力)这一术语,主要考虑到两个方面的原因:一是本书主要针对初步探索跨文化能力的读者,暂时不宜引介易引起混淆的相似概念做深入的学术讨论,从而方便初学者理解和掌握概貌;二是学界与此相关的各种术语比较纷杂,如跨文化交际能力(intercultural communicative competence)、文化间性(interculturality)、多元文化交际能力(multicultural competence)、多样化应对能力(diversity competence)等,而"intercultural competence"一直被学者提及和使用,这个概念可以涵盖各种细分的界定,也方便统一表述书中涉及的、人们日常生活中常见的各种跨文化交流能力。

(2) 国内外学者对跨文化能力构成因素和解决途径的规定多有重叠或侧重,而一些词汇如"尊重"(respect)、"开放"(openness)等,编写者认为在中文语境中不能简单地把它们归为是动机、心态、认知、技巧、行为中的某一种,可能是其中两种或多种,因此跨文化能力每个构成因素本身并不容易被清晰地界定,彼此之间在时间顺序上也没有必然的逻辑关联。但是,对于每个进入、体验、应对和反思一个具体的跨文化过程的个体来说,这些构成因素仍然会形成某种时空上的逻辑联系,具有基本的时间和空间顺序。本书认为跨文化冲突的处理就是这样一个"过程",暂且称之为"跨文化通道"(**intercultural tunnel**),并依此来设置各单元的讨论话题,其基本脉络如下:意识到进入一个"跨文化通道"——松动身心——避免过度概括——延迟判断——多角度持续探索——体会移情和尊重——因地制宜地协调——调整文化身份和价值观念——反观、衡量和提升。

其中"松动"(looseness/loosening up)这一概念来源于东方的哲学思考,在西方学者跨文化研究中也有提及(如哲学家、汉学家佛朗索瓦·于连和物理学家戴维·玻姆)。但本书把它编入最初始的实际操作单元,认为它是交流者心态、认知、行为、态度在跨文化时空中对外发生连接的撬动点,同时它又贯穿整个跨文化交流过程的始终,是在交流中产生积极能量的保证。

（3）本书依据"个体实用和操作原则"，重点关注如何解决真实的、个体化的跨文化交流中产生的负面感受，如紧张、焦虑、不适、反感、仇恨、受辱等，认为这才是人们在实际中谈论和训练跨文化能力的主要目的。**因此，本书缩短了理论概述和讨论，增加了与一般读者的互动体验。**对于每个主题的互动部分，本书直接采用课堂教学实践和社会生活实践中人们的真实、鲜活、平实的案例作为编写素材（人名为化名）。

（4）**本书依然提供部分段落的理论探讨、思考性话题、互动小锦囊、援引阅读和详细的文献信息，供有专业兴趣的读者深入研究。**但书中理论探讨部分并不囿于某些繁琐的概念或某一种跨文化构成模式，也并不完全对应跨文化研究理论的基本脉络，而是拣选对大家较为实用的理论进行介绍。一些学术概念为方便读者理解进行了简化、概括或释义性书写，但所引皆有据可考，并尽可能谨守其定义和内涵。

三、鸣谢

本书的援引阅读部分，撷思想精华于各位文学、语言学、人类学、社会学、心理学等领域的前辈或同行，是我们钻研前行的引导和借鉴，编写团队向他们表示衷心的敬意和感谢！

同时，编写团队衷心感谢比利时鲁汶大学 Jan Van Maele 教授为本书提供理论指导、内容顾问并分享相关资料；感谢南京大学英语系丁言仁教授常年不遗余力地指导和鼓励；感谢杭州电子科技大学王一安教授为本书的编写提供建议；同时感谢南京大学出版社董颖老师和我们多年的精诚合作，她对本书的出版予以充分肯定和全力支持；感谢 Julia Hofmann 女士对每个章节的英文修改工作以及其先生 Albrecht Hofmann 教授对英文序言的修改。

本书编写过程中，我们邀请了具有跨文化教学经验和翻译经验的南京大学金陵学院英语专业杨芸老师和王欣老师分别完成了 1～4 节和 5～8 节的翻译工作。2015、2016、2017、2018 级英语专业部分同学参与了资料的整理、翻译、语言润色、配图等工作，这也是师生共同学习、丰富编写视角、突出学习者需求的一次实践和探索。参与编写的同学们是（按姓氏拼音字母顺序）：

陈佳平　代译姝　姜　楠　赖慧伶　李晓瑶　倪德芝　钱于昊　盛名洋　谭舒尹
汤舒雅　王淑娴　韦诗颖　吴雨馨　叶嘉琪　张　友　赵　婧　郑博凡　周柳余

在此向他们表示衷心的感谢！

于　群
2020 年 5 月于南京玄武湖畔

Preface

Ⅰ. Ideals, trust, and efforts

Nowadays globalization has greatly increased the mobility of people living in different parts of the world. They are exposed, consciously or unconsciously, to other languages, cultural customs and values, thus they encounter all kinds of "other cultures" and enter culturally hybridized contexts.

There is an old saying: it is easier said than done. Many people may be familiar with the term "intercultural competence", and have more or less experienced cultural differences, but they sometimes suffer from anxiety, hesitation, worries, and uncomfortableness during cultural contacts with people of other cultures. The main reason behind this might be that they have not managed cultural differences well enough with proper skills and strategies, nor do they believe that people, to a great extent, are willing and able to comfortably, pleasantly, and creatively make joint efforts to solve the conflicts arising from cultural differences. Globally, differences in cultural beliefs and identities may even lead to devastating conflicts such as wars or racial massacres.

Although this book tries to solve some cultural conflicts such as quarrels, fighting, or clashes, all the discussions and interactive trainings in the book are based on a trust that people in this world can communicate with good will and sincerity. The author tries to help the individual to avoid embarrassment and pain when encountering cultural conflicts, not by thorough and systematic theoretical discussion from the perspective of scholars, but by arranging themes and contents from the perspective of the actual needs of the readers. It is hoped that while learning some basic concepts and theories about intercultural competence, the readers can also participate in the interaction parts of the book to practice necessary skills with the scenarios provided. It is hoped that after a period of practicing, the readers can enjoy a more comfortable communication with people with other cultural beliefs and values.

Though on many occasions people don't need to "sell their souls" or to "give up their bottom lines" to gain an effective intercultural communication, we still realize that a more profound and more effective communication often lies in dialogues between different cultural values. Yet to loosen the values people have been adhering to as the foundation of their identities sounds almost like a mission impossible. However, this is exactly the first step of opening a dialogue which will in the end modify, extend, and enrich one's original values to some extent. Thus it needs an "effort impossible". As Dean Rickles writes in the foreword for Bohm in *On Dialogue* (2014): "(For this reason Bohmian dialogue) requires effort—it is an active procedure, demanding a level of self-denial and ego elimination akin to Buddhism."

Some readers might think it too simple and idealistic, or a cliché, to still talk about respect, empathy and delay of judgment. Some scholars may also hold the same views. They either find the development of intercultural competence is too closely related to cultural values, cultural identities, and power games, or they find that communication is certainly constrained by the interlocutors' personalities and psychology in different contexts, so keeping to talk about respect, empathy or delaying judgment may not substantially help build up the intercultural competence. However, the author of this book believes these "ideal" elements are still very much essential and necessary for an individual who is in a "dark tunnel". Even all kinds of interfering elements are considered seriously, these "ideal" elements are well worth striving for.

II. Some thoughts on the composition of this book

This book mainly tries to answer the following questions:

》 What is culture? What is intercultural competence?
》 What are the crucial and practical steps in obtaining skills and strategies to develop intercultural competence?
》 How is the assessment of intercultural competence possible?

This book is based on the following thinking:

(1) The author uses "intercultural competence" as an umbrella term throughout nine themes instead of using other terminologies, e.g., intercultural communicative competence, interculturality, diversity competence, or multicultural competence, which the author finds overlapping in connotations, thus might be too confusing for those who are exposed to theories related to intercultural competence for the first time.

(2) To date there are many conceptions and definitions related to cultural differences and communication competences. They are either overlapping or focusing more on certain aspects than others in connotation. Some "components", such as respect, or openness, according to the author, cannot be simply categorized as an attitude, a cognitive skill, or a behavior. They might be two or more of these "components" at the same time. Therefore the author finds it hard to draw clear boundaries between such components. At the same

time, the author finds that **basically people can still discuss these "components" in a chronological way in practice.** In fact, in each individual intercultural conflict, a person still literally goes through a "process" (see more discussion in theme 2.2), from facing an intercultural conflict to experiencing it, to solving or retreating from the conflict and to reflecting on it later on. We simulate this process as an "intercultural tunnel". The sequential nine steps in this intercultural tunnel, which form the nine themes in the book, are as follows:

→being aware of entering an intercultural tunnel
→loosening up and opening up
→avoiding over-generalization
→delaying the judgment
→exploring from multiple perspectives
→being empathetic and respectful
→constructing dynamic cultures and solving the problems contextually
→constructing and adjusting identities dynamically
→reflecting and assessing intercultural competences

"Looseness" is an important concept in old oriental philosophies and is not much highlighted in intercultural research. This book sees this concept as important and discusses it at the very moment when entering "the intercultural tunnel". The author believes that it is the key step that can appraise every possible communication and can drive the affects, attitudes, skills, and behaviors of an interlocutor to possibly connect with each other. It goes through the "intercultural tunnel" and generates the positive initiatives during the communication.

(3) As mentioned before, this book is not written from the perspective of scholars but from the perspective of the users and readers. It focuses on how to rid an individual of the negative feelings when encountering cultural conflicts, such as nervousness, anxiety, inadequacy, hatred, or insult. The author believes that mastering skills for tackling these feelings in practice is crucial, thus it has become such an important part in developing intercultural competence. Therefore, **this book has shortened the lengthy theoretical discussions and increased the practical interaction sections.** Many scenarios provided in the interaction sections are collected from people's daily lives (with aliases).

(4) **The book still leaves enough room for readers who are driven by academic interests; it includes some paragraphs of more detailed theoretical introductions, reflective questions, toolkits for interaction, quoted readings as well as citations and references.** However, the theoretical sections are not led by an attempt to introduce

sophisticated and sometimes chaotic concepts, nor do they follow only one model of intercultural competence. Instead, they are intended to simplify, generalize, or interpret those concepts for the convenience of readers on the basis of being faithful to their original connotations and being strict in citations and references.

Ⅲ. Acknowledgements

Some texts in the "quoted readings" are quoted from books and papers written by forerunners in the fields of literature, linguistics, sociology, psychology, or anthropology, to whom the composition team of this book pay great tribute. These masterpieces illuminate our way to creating better solutions to human conflicts like beacons standing by the misty sea of ignorance. Some other quotations are from books and papers of colleagues. We extends great gratitude to them. Their writing is full of wisdom derived from strenuous academic work.

The composition team extend our great gratitude to Prof. Jan Van Maele from KU Leuven, who has provided theoretical guidance, content consultation, and research materials without reservation. We also thank Prof. Stephen Ding from Nanjing University, who has always been encouraging and supporting our research. We should also thank Mrs. Julia Hofmann and Prof. Albrecht Hofmann, for their hard work in revision of the English texts in every theme. We are grateful to Prof. Wang Yi'an, from Hangzhou Electronic Technology University for his invaluable suggestions and discussions of the contents of the book. We thank Ms. Dong Ying, Chief Editor of Nanjing University Press, for her all-year round guidance and support to make the publication of this book possible.

We thank Ms. Yang Yun and Ms. Wang Xin, experienced teachers from Nanjing University Jinling College, who translated themes 1 – 4 and 5 – 8 respectively into English. We must also thank students from the English Department in our school for collecting, sorting out, and working on the materials and the pictures. This is an attempt to integrate more perspectives from the users to enhance the applied aspects of this book. This is also an opportunity for teachers and students to work together and probe knowledge more deeply. The names of these students are (in alphabet order):

Chen Jiaping	Dai Yishu	Jiang Nan	Lai Huiling	Li Xiaoyao
Ni Dezhi	Qian Yuhao	Sheng Mingyang	Tan Shuyin	Tang Shuya
Wang Shuxian	Wei Shiying	Wu Yuxin	Ye Jiaqi	Zhang You
Zhao Jing	Zheng Bofan	Zhou Liuyu		

Sharry Yu
May, 2020
Xuanwu Lake, Nanjing

内容使用指导

本书采用中英双语编写，方便不同专业、不同英语程度的读者使用。对于每个单元的理论探讨和互动环节，使用者可以根据不同需求灵活取用，也可以改编使用。每个单元的援引阅读部分，也包含中文和英文两种阅读素材。

本书可适用的人群包括：

- 中学和大学里学习英语、汉语语言和文学、社会学、人类学、传播学等学科的学生
- 出国进行短期交流和长期学习的中国留学生
- 来中国进行短期交流和长期学习的外国留学生
- 出国旅行或工作的中国人
- 来中国旅行或工作的外国朋友
- 身处各种多元文化环境里的各类人士

本书共设九节，每节围绕一个话题从两个方面进行讨论，每个方面都由"理论引介"和"互动与体验"两大板块组成，其中，理论板块又附"思考与讨论"和"互动小锦囊"两个环节。此外，每节篇末还设有"援引阅读"。各章节话题具体内容见"目录"。每个环节的具体设计意图和使用方法介绍如下：

理论引介：这个部分尽量提纲挈领、深入浅出地概括和介绍跨文化能力提升步骤中涉及的主要概念及背景知识。让初次接触跨文化系统理论的读者一目了然，从而对后面的互动练习有所指引，但又不会让他们深陷其中，感到迷雾重重，或者觉得老生常谈，索然无味。对理论不感兴趣的读者可以对这部分做简要了解后，进入后面的"互动与体验"环节。对这个学科有更浓厚兴趣的读者，可以进入"思考与讨论"环节和"援引阅读"环节，并循着"参考文献"做深入的学习。教师在使用时，可以根据自身教学需求和学生的具体情况来掌握对这些理论介绍的难度和深度。

思考与讨论：这个部分给出三个与前面理论引介部分相关的思考或讨论话题。这些问题大部分都是开放性的，没有具体统一的答案：一来是因为在这个学科领域内不少问题都还在探讨摸索中；二来这也是契合了跨文化能力的本来精神——思考、对话和促进。读者可以跟自己的同学、朋友、家人共同探讨这些问题。课堂上老师学生们也可以选取这些问题进行即兴地讨论。

这些话题后面，还给出空间让读者们在阅读和讨论后进行反思，并提出自己的

问题。

互动小锦囊："互动小锦囊"采用形象、简洁、直观的方式,如表格、模拟图、流程图等,来展现某一个理论具体的观点、内涵、思路或风貌。它起到承上启下的作用:一方面与前面介绍的理论相关联,起到补充作用;一方面与后面的互动练习相关联,起到指引作用,其内容会在后面互动环节中有所体现和深化。

互动与体验:这个环节是欢迎读者们在对相关理论有了一定的了解之后,返回到真实活泼的日常生活中,通过积极地互动、体验、感受和分析,来更深入地理解跨文化能力的内涵,并在心态、知识、技能、策略等各方面真正提升跨文化能力。这些互动练习既可以为读者自学使用,也可以作为课堂练习使用。

援引阅读:每个章节的末尾,我们援引了编写过程中涉及的参考文献里与章节内容相关的段落。这些援引段落如一颗颗珍珠或一块块玉佩,闪烁着先人、前辈们思想的光辉和同行研究者们的思想精华,它们或者是对文中某个理论概念的完整表述,或者是对某种思想的旁征佐引,它们拓展了每个章节的理论背景和思想范畴,指引有兴趣的读者阅读原文,掌握思想发展本身的缘起和内在的天然联系。

How to use this book

The book is composed bilingually in both Chinese and English, so that people in different intercultural contexts can use it. Teachers, students, travelers, or scholars can make flexible use of the parts and sections in each theme.

The users and readers of this book may include:

- Students who are learning Chinese language and literature, English language and literature, sociology, anthropology, and communication in middle schools or universities
- Chinese students for short-term or long-term study outside China
- Foreign students coming to China for short-term or long-term study
- Chinese citizens who travel or work aboard
- Travelers coming to China from other parts of the world
- People who are in any multi-cultural environment (schools, companies, organizations, etc.)

The nine themes in this book are each divided into two sections (see "Table of Contents"). Each section has the following parts:

Introduction

This part holds brief discussions, mostly theoretically on the background and connotations of the skills in practical steps in intercultural competence development, as well as how the skill in one theme is connected with skills introduced in other themes. This part provides necessary knowledge and guidance for the readers to practice in the "interaction" part later on. Those who are more driven by academic interests may go to "questions for reflection", and "quoted readings" in each theme and then "references" in the Appendix to further explore the related research around the theme. Teachers using this book may arrange the teaching contents according to the students' interests and foundation.

Reflection and discussion

This part provides three open questions for reflection and discussion on the theoretical explanation given in the "Introduction". There are no specific answers to these questions because they are either still controversially discussed by researchers, or because they are intended to invite the readers to explore their own life experiences. Readers can keep on discussing them with their classmates, friends and family members, which is exactly the true spirit of intercultural communication that this book is advocating. Teachers in the classroom can arrange group discussions or even debates with these questions. The author also leaves space for readers to raise their own questions or write down their own reflections in this part.

Toolkits for interaction

This part gives a visual introduction to a concept, a method, or a structure in intercultural competence development by a chart, a diagram, a figure, or a picture. It supplements the theories introduced before and at the same time prepares the readers to enter the interactions that follow. Its content will be integrated deeper and understood better with the readers practicing more in the "interaction" part.

Interaction

This part shows how the author of the book highlights the practical aspect in intercultural competence development. Three interactive exercises are designed in each section of each theme, so there are altogether 54 in this book. It is hoped that readers can participate actively in this part—going back to their own lives to practice with new skills in more intercultural communication after understanding the theories, and then feel the true changes. These interactive exercises can be done either by autonomous learners or by teachers and students in the classrooms. Some exercises are not strictly designed in intercultural contexts, but they still lead to the development of intercultural competence.

Quoted readings

This part presents some highlights, some in Chinese and some in English, of the broader readings done by the author when composing the book. The quoted texts can guide readers to a deeper understanding of the origins and development of some theories on the basis of which this book is written. Sometimes these thoughts interact or reflect on each other from different times and different intellectual realms, so in the end the readers will realize that some human thoughts, though different on the surface, are actually advancing in the same direction.

目 录

第一节　什么是跨文化能力？我们为什么要培养它？
1.1　什么是跨文化能力？ ·· 2
1.2　我们为什么要培养跨文化能力？ ································· 10

第二节　松动身心，意识到自己正进入"跨文化通道"
2.1　让身心松动 ·· 20
2.2　意识到自己正在进入"跨文化通道" ······························ 26

第三节　利用概括性知识，同时打破固化刻板的思维
3.1　概括性知识的利用和慎用 ··· 40
3.2　非文化本质主义的观念和行为 ··································· 48

第四节　延迟判断，应对"模糊性"
4.1　延迟你的判断 ··· 60
4.2　应对"模糊性" ··· 67

第五节　多角度了解信息和认知问题
5.1　多角度了解信息 ·· 80
5.2　多角度认知问题 ·· 86

第六节　移情与尊重
6.1　体会移情 ··· 98
6.2　真正做到尊重 ·· 106

第七节　动态地建构文化，因地制宜解决问题
7.1　"建构"一种文化 ··· 118

7.2　因地制宜解决问题 ·· 124

第八节　动态的文化身份和柔韧的文化疆界
　　8.1　动态地建构和调适文化身份 ····································· 136
　　8.2　建构柔韧的文化疆界 ·· 143

第九节　反思和衡量你的跨文化能力
　　9.1　跨文化能力测试必要性和标准的讨论 ······················· 156
　　9.2　结合多种手段来衡量跨文化能力 ······························ 164

参考文献 ·· 175

Contents

Theme 1　Development of intercultural competence

　1.1　Understanding intercultural competence ·················· 2

　1.2　Developing your intercultural competence ·················· 10

Theme 2　Looseness and the awareness of the "intercultural tunnel"

　2.1　Loosening up ·················· 20

　2.2　Being aware of the "intercultural tunnel" ·················· 26

Theme 3　Generalization and non-essentialist perspectives

　3.1　Generalizing and over-generalizing ·················· 40

　3.2　Understanding non-essentialist perspectives ·················· 48

Theme 4　Delaying judgment and managing ambiguity

　4.1　Delaying your judgment ·················· 60

　4.2　Managing ambiguity ·················· 67

Theme 5　Multi-perspective exploring and understanding

　5.1　Exploring with multiple perspectives ·················· 80

　5.2　Understanding with multi-perspectives ·················· 86

Theme 6　Empathy and respect

　6.1　Experiencing empathy ·················· 98

　6.2　Being truly respectful ·················· 106

Theme 7　Culture construction and contextual problem-solving

　7.1　"Constructing" a culture ·················· 118

7.2　Solving the problems contextually ········· 124

Theme 8　Dynamic cultural identities and pliable cultural boundaries

8.1　Constructing and adjusting cultural identities dynamically ········· 136

8.2　Constructing pliable cultural boundaries ········· 143

Theme 9　Reflections and assessments on your IC

9.1　IC assessment: difficult yet necessary ········· 156

9.2　Assessing IC with combination of different methods ········· 164

References ········· 175

第一节
什么是跨文化能力？我们为什么要培养它？

Theme 1
Development of intercultural competence

第一节 什么是跨文化能力？我们为什么要培养它？
Theme 1　Development of intercultural competence

1.1　什么是跨文化能力？
Understanding intercultural competence

理论引介 Introduction

说起文化，它好像是个再普通不过的字眼儿。它无处不在，我们都能谈论文化上的一些事儿。"跨文化"这个概念，我们好像也能说出一些东西来。但文化（culture）的内涵到底是什么呢？跨文化能力（intercultural competence）又是什么呢？对文化的理解和对跨文化能力的理解其实是相辅相成的。因此，我们先从"文化"说起。

关于什么是文化，人们给出了很多不同的定义。有些学者认为争论到底什么是文化、或者不断完善文化这个概念的定义不是最首要的任务。但编者认为综合一些学者提出的基本的文化特性，还是必要的。这些特性包括以下几点：

（1）文化是指某一个团体中占据主导的、习惯性的认知或行为（而不是个别的、暂时的现象）；

（2）文化是社会生活中习得（而不是生物性、遗传性的）的方面；

（3）文化具有多种形式，包括语言、文字、艺术、服饰、风俗、价值观念、社会规约、历史文化认知、法律和政治制度等；

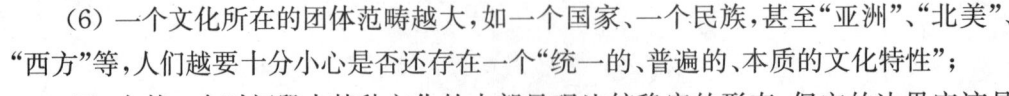

（4）文化在不同的社会团体中有不同的内容，因此两种文化之间既具有相似性，也具有差异性，但并没有某个居于中心或在很大程度上优越于其它文化的文化；

（5）一种文化具有一些主导或基本的特征，但这些特征并不像自然科学物种的特性那样具有高度的一致性和排他性，文化内部具有多样性（multiplicity）和异质性（heterogeneity）；

（6）一个文化所在的团体范畴越大，如一个国家、一个民族，甚至"亚洲"、"北美"、"西方"等，人们越要十分小心是否还存在一个"统一的、普遍的、本质的文化特性"；

（7）在某一个时间段内某种文化的内部呈现比较稳定的形态，但它的边界应该是柔韧的,要不断靠和其它文化的交流得以生成、创造和丰润。

基于对文化的种种理解,学者们开始定义跨文化能力(Intercultural Competence,简称IC)这个概念。但各国学者出于不同的需要或侧重不同的理论视野,目前给出了至少49种定义(Deardorff,2006:242)。对于构成跨文化能力的因素,他们也有不同的描述,包括对某种文化形态的知识、跨文化经历者的心态、动机、行为、意识等。这些归类有的粗略有的细腻,有的重叠或各有侧重,再加上采用内涵不尽相同的中文对应词汇,更是精彩纷呈。而且,跨文化能力和跨文化交际能力、第二语言交际能力之间的关系也仍然在研究和探讨过程中。

但是,这些并不意味着无法解释或理解这样一种能力。我们在这里给出意大利学者Borghetti(2017)的一个理解。为方便阅读,我们把这个定义分为下面三个层次:

(1) 跨文化能力是人们从总体上理解另一个不同文化现象并与之互动的能力,包括人们在这一过程中的认知、心态和行为等方面的能力。

(2) 这些能力可以通过教育以及(或者)个人体验来得到发展。

(3) 跨文化能力与人们在跨文化互动中如何确认自己在社会中的种种身份有关(比如根据自己的国籍还是性别、年龄、社会地位,等等),与他们是否能

意识到自己如何确认这些身份有关,也与他们有意愿、有能力承认他人具有多重身份并与之协调有关(如同他们确认自己的身份那样)。

在讨论跨文化能力这个概念时,大家也同时在探讨文化差异(cultural difference)、认同(identity)、中心主义(centrism)、多样性(diversity)、对话(dialogue)、文化间性(interculturality)、非文化本质主义(non-essentialism,见本书4.2部分)、身份管理(identity management)、共文化(co-culture)等相关的概念,试图更深入地理解有关跨文化(the intercultural)的现象、过程、因素和内涵。

跨文化能力的种种定义和认知的理论来源,包括社会学、现代传播学、社会心理学、认知心理学和后现代主义中的多元主义、解构主义、建构主义、身份认同、他者等。跨文化能力发展中,涉及的一个关键概念是文化认同。文化认同既可以是一个与政治、历史相关的"大"概念,也可以是一个和个人性格、心理相关的"小"概念。

学者Hall提出了"相似趋同轴"(the axis of similarity and continuity)以及"相异迷思轴"(the axis of difference and rapture)两个认同维度(1990:226)。中国学者戴晓东认为,跨文化过程中的文化认同现象,即有向其独特性延伸的向度,也有对外开放调适、向普遍性延伸的向度(2013:148)。学者Starosta提出类似的说法,他认为某个"中心"(the centrism),在作为某种特定文化时可以延续数代,而作为某种社会团体,它

对自身的坚持会发生变化。(2010:53)

受到后现代主义的影响,很多学者强调跨文化过程的"动态建构"的特征,他们希望更多人能看到这一过程具有"能动性"和"创造性",从而积极地去解决问题,促成和解或合作。与此同时,一些学者也提出跨文化能力受到权力、个人性格等因素的制约而是否可以定义、学习或测试的问题。(Dervin,2017;Borghetti,2017)

To know what intercultural competence is, it is reasonable to start from what culture is and what characteristics it has. The understanding of intercultural competence accumulates along with the understanding of culture.

Scholars domestic and abroad give many different definitions of "culture". Some believe that the primary task is not to argue what culture is or to continually perfect the definition of culture. Nevertheless, it is still quite necessary to list some features that culture presents. Here is a summary of how "culture" has been characterized in literature:

i. Culture refers to the dominant, habitual (not individual or temporary) cognitions or behaviour of a certain social group.

ii. Culture refers to aspects that people acquire in social life (not to biological or hereditary aspects).

iii. It exists in many forms, including language, words, arts, clothes, customs, values, social norms, perception of history and culture, legislation, and political systems, etc.

iv. Cultures differ from one another. Both similarities and differences can be found between two cultures. However, to a great extent, a certain culture cannot stay in the centre or be superior to other cultures.

v. A culture has some relatively essential or general features, but they are not as highly coherent and exclusive as those found in a biological species. A culture of a group is characterized by multiplicity and heterogeneity within that group.

vi. The larger domain a certain culture is in, such as a country, a nation, or even "Asia", "North America", "the West" and so on, the more careful we should be about the "unified, common, or essential characteristics".

vii. In a certain period a culture remains internally stable, but still with flexible, pliable boundaries. Some new parts of a culture are created and enriched through continuous exchanges of living experiences with other cultures.

Based on the understandings of culture, scholars have defined the concept of Intercultural Competence (IC for short). Because of different demands or emphases on diverse theoretical scopes, experts have put forward at least 49 definitions on IC (Deardorff, 2006: 242). Researchers give different descriptions to the components of IC, including cognition of a certain culture, such as psychology, affection, motivation, behavior, and awareness of the interlocutors, and so on. Rude or minute, overlapping or emphasizing, together with the difficulties caused by translation, these explanations might make things more confusing rather than clarifying. Furthermore, the relationship between intercultural competence, the intercultural communicative competence and linguistic competence of second language is still under research and discussion. However, it doesn't mean that we cannot explain or understand intercultural competence. Here we take Claudia Borgetti's understanding of IC as following (2017):

> IC is conceived here as an integral whole of cognitive, affective and behavioural factors that influence the understanding of, and interaction with, diversity in a broad sense, and which can be developed through education and/or experience.[...] Intercultural competence is thus linked to how individuals socially position themselves in interactions (e.g., according to their nationality, genre, age, social status, etc.), to their awareness of such positioning, and to their willingness and ability to recognise and negotiate the others' multiple identities as much as their own.

While discussing intercultural competence, scholars also probe into other concepts like cultural difference, identity, centrism, diversity, dialogue, interculturality, non-essentialism, identity management, and co-culture, in the hope of further understanding a variety of phenomena, processes, factors and implications concerning "the intercultural".

Theoretical origins of the diverse definitions and cognitions of intercultural competence include pluralism, post-modernism, deconstructionism, and constructivism, modern communication, social psychology, and cognitive psychology, etc. One of the key concepts in developing intercultural competence is cultural identity. Cultural identity can be related to politics and history as well as to a person's personality and psychology.

Stuart Hall puts forward two dimensions of cultural identity: "the axis of similarity and continuity" and "the axis of difference and rapture" (1990:226). Chinese scholar Dai Xiaodong believes that cultural identity is not only extending inwardly to the dimension of its uniqueness, but also opens to the dimension outwardly to its general features (2013:148). William Starosta puts forward a similar theory, which says that "the centrism" can last several generations as a certain culture but a certain cultural group will change its insistence in some of its values. (2010:53)

Some other scholars emphasize the "dynamic construction" of the cultures during the processes of intercultural communication. They hope the communicators can see the more dynamic and constructive aspects of IC, so that they can become more creative and initiative in solving problems during the communication or cooperation. In the meantime, some scholars began to argue about whether intercultural competence could be defined, studied, or tested at all, for example, because of the restriction of power and personal characters. (e.g., Dervin, 2017; Borghetti, 2017)

第一节 什么是跨文化能力？我们为什么要培养它？
Theme 1 Development of intercultural competence

思考 & 讨论 Reflection and discussion

1. 一个国家的政治制度和法律制度是否属于文化的范畴呢？
2. 怎样来理解"中国人春节喜欢吃饺子"这个历史悠久的文化风俗所具有的"柔韧的边界"？（请参考 1.1 中对于文化特性的介绍）
3. 哪些情况下一个团体要保持既有的文化，哪些情况下需要"改良"既有的文化？

1. Do political and legislative systems of a country fall within the ambit of culture?
2. How to understand the pliable, dynamic boundary of the traditional custom of eating dumplings on Chinese Spring Festival holidays (see "features of culture" in 1.1.)?
3. Can you give some examples to illustrate under what circumstance a group should preserve some established cultural customs and under what they should modify and amend them?

学习者自己的提问和反思 Your own questions and reflections

1. _____
   _____
2. _____
   _____
3. _____
   _____

互动小锦囊 Toolkits for interaction

综合前面提到的文化的种种特性，我们不妨画出这样一个文化的形态——它的核心地带具有比较稳定的、让其成员有归属感的较为统一的价值观和行为方式；同时，又不断与外界其它文化价值观和行为方式相遇，产生交流，适时地、动态地根据不同的目的进行调整，在边界地带具有开放的、柔软的、流动互通的特性，最终整个文化体的外延不断得以伸展，内涵不断得以滋润和丰厚。

Integrating the characteristics of culture mentioned above, a culture can be presented vividly as below—in the central area lie commonly shared values and norms which bring the sense of belonging to its members and help with the self identification. Meanwhile, it encounters and communicates with other cultural values and norms and then mediates and adapts dynamically in different contexts so that in the outer area the culture is characterized with openness, flexibility, hybridity and interaction. Seen over a long period, this culture is externally extensive and internally enriched.

一个社会团体的"文化",它的中心较为稳定,边界地带始终活跃
The culture of a social group, with relatively stable, commonly shared values and norms in the central area, and with dynamic interactions in the border area

  互动&体验 Interaction

1. 我们来体验一下一种"常规的判断"其实可能并不一定那么"常规"。(第一个例子已经给出):

(1) 白人都挺有钱的。这个进店的客户是白人,我要跟他多聊聊,让他买个LV包。

但还有不少这样的情况:

——由于经济发展状况不佳,一些国家的白人生活困难,买一个LV包并不是一件容易的事。

——不同白人对金钱的态度是不同的,有的白人即使很有钱,也不一定会把钱花在奢侈品上。

——"白人"的定义非常困难,从基因学、人类学角度都有不同的定义。

(2) 印度脏乱差,干嘛要去那里玩!

但还有不少这样的情况:

- _____
- _____
- _____

(3) 中国妇女吃苦耐劳，勤奋节俭。我娶个中国媳妇，有福了！
但还有不少这样的情况：
- _____
- _____
- _____

4) 欧洲人对人平等尊重。
但还有不少这样的情况：
- _____
- _____
- _____

2. 一位"西方文化"课的主讲老师第一次上课时问学生："你觉得西方文化有哪些特征？"这个提问分别有什么恰当和不恰当的地方吗？

3. 文化具有穿越国界和民族边界的特征。同样的文化观念可以发生在不同国家的家庭里，不同的文化观念也可以发生在同一个家庭不同人身上。例如以下这些关于儿女与父母关系的描述。

在德国的一个普通家庭里，有三个孩子。大儿子非常独立，不需要家里贴补生活、帮忙带孩子。二儿子和妈妈经常争吵，但和父母见面很多，会请父母帮忙修电灯和水管，参与装修房子。三女儿不结婚，也不生孩子，有一个同居二十年的男友。在中国，很多家庭里的儿女会请父母帮忙照顾自己的孩子，也有很多子女住在外地，和父母关系疏远；有的子女是丁克一族，或者一直不结婚。

你生活里有没有 1~2 个类似的文化现象？

1. Let's try to find out how the failure of realizing cultural diversity and heterogeneity influence our everyday thinking. (The first example is given.)

i. White people are rich. The customer who is now entering our shop is a white man. I'm going to talk with him a lot and try to sell him a Louis Vuitton bag.

But these situations also exist:

— Due to the economic slump in some countries, some white people are living a difficult life. It is no easy thing for them to buy a Louis Vuitton bag.

— Different white people hold different attitudes towards money. Some refuse to spend money on luxuries in spite of being rich.

— People who identify themselves as a "white man" may not be recognized as such by certain groups in certain contexts.

ii. India is a rat hole. Why do you want to travel there?

But these situations also exist:
- _____
- _____
- _____

iii. Chinese women are hardy, diligent, and frugal. I am very lucky to marry a Chinese woman!

But these situations also exist:
- _____
- _____
- _____

iv. Europeans are respectful and enjoy a high level of equality.

But these situations also exist:
- _____
- _____
- _____

2. A lecturer who teaches a course of "Western Culture" asks the students during the first class: "What are the characteristics of the Western Culture?" In what aspects do you think the question is appropriate and/or inappropriate?

3. Culture goes beyond the boundaries of countries and nationalities. The same cultural value can be found in different families in different countries. Likewise, different cultural values can be found in different members of the same family. Take the perception of parent-kid relationship for example:

An ordinary German family has three children. The eldest son is very independent. He never expects subsidies from his parents or their help for looking after his children. The second son quarrels a lot with his mother but he also meets his parents more frequently than the eldest son. He sometimes asks his parents to help fix the lights and drains or even asks for parents' advice on house decorations. The youngest daughter doesn't want to get married or have a child. She has a boyfriend whom she has lived with for twenty years.

In China, it is common for grandparents to take care of grandchildren. Whereas some children live far away from their parents thus they are quite estranged from their parents. Some Chinese young couples are DINK or they don't want to get married.

Can you find one or two similar cultural phenomena in your life?

1.2 我们为什么要提高跨文化能力?
Developing your intercultural competence

 理论引介 Introduction

遭遇跨文化冲突时,并不是只能敬而远之。

从上面对跨文化能力的定义,我们可以尝试探究一下为什么要提高跨文化能力。普通中国公民在走出国门旅行、学习和工作时,或者在国内各种多元文化环境中进行交流、合作、谈判等活动时,大家在欣喜兴奋的同时也可能经历过一些不顺、不快、困扰、误会和烦恼,甚至发生争执,诉诸法律,引发冲突。这就是跨文化冲突。跨文化冲突是指"来自两种文化的双方在内容、认同、关系和过程等方面所主观认为的(或实际发生了的)在价值观、规范、处理方式、目标上的互不相容。"(Ting-Toomey, 2007:194)

那么,我们是不是在具有文化上差异的情境中,就只能束手无策、被动忍受或敬而远之呢?

是不是我们和具有不同文化价值观的人交往,就没有办法更加深入?我们和他们的矛盾就没有办法解决?

是不是多年深厚的社会、历史、民族等原因导致我们完全误解,只能互相敬而远之或听之任之?

我们不能轻易地说不,放弃努力。在很多情况下,我们可以通过学习跨文化能力的基本知识和技能来更积极勇敢地化解不适,解决矛盾。

遭遇跨文化冲突时,也并不是只能表面一团和气或转而抨击。 还有一些人认为,自己脾气挺好,与人为善,一般不与人发生冲突,跨文化能力学习离自己很远。但其实跨文化意识和能力的薄弱隐藏在我们平日点点滴滴的言行里。我们来听听身边的人经常说的话:

"我才不要找个外国男朋友呢,他们都长得好奇怪!"

"金窝银窝不如自己的狗窝!还是家门口最自在啊!"

"那个老外不跟你结婚?你被骗了!"

"那个老外一到酒店就问我们城市里有没有红灯区(白眼)。"

大家是否意识到,上面说到的这些负面感受,其实是由很多因素导致和构成的。通过这本书的学习和练习,我们可以了解导致这些感受的深层次原因,尤其是可以逐渐意识到,良好的跨文化互动需要积极的动机引导,需要人们有勇气突破自己的性情和价值观,突破内心的心理障碍和外界的权力障碍,然后去积极建构新的认识,寻求协调方案的过程。

并不是了解了别人的文化,我们就有了跨文化能力,就可以舒适、有效地交流。我们曾经学习了不少关于其它国家或民族的文化。比如美国文化,我们可能了解得最多。但为什么我们那么多朋友或孩子去了美国,总是因为文化障碍产生焦虑、和别人发生矛盾呢?由此我们应该意识到,了解了其它文化的知识内容本身,并不意味着能完全帮助我们舒适、有效地交流和协调关系。因为一个"特定"的交流过程,涉及"特定"的交流者双方"特定"的文化价值观、"特定"的身份、"特定"的外部环境、当时"特定"的心态和情绪等多种因素影响。怎样去认识这些"特定"的因素,怎样去适时地利用和协调它们,是跨文化能力提升中比较关键的内容。

在平衡利弊之后,因地制宜地采用跨文化策略。积极勇敢的跨文化诉求也可能受很多因素的干扰而被放弃,这是正常的。我们并不是一味地鼓励人们要不断冲破原有的价值立场和个人性格,不考虑周遭环境。相反,我们想鼓励人们在全面平衡"接纳新文化的付出"与"从新文化中获得新奇视角和内心喜悦"的情况下,来尝试培养跨文化意识和心态,因地制宜地调解不适,只要大家能感受到在有些情况下,还可能找到和以往不同的、更好的观察视角和解决方案,就很好了。

因此,在提高跨文化能力过程中,除了学习其它文化的基本知识,还需要去了解整个跨文化过程到底发生了什么,需要学习一些技巧去顺利进入这个过程,调适各种因素,最大化地完成双方交流的目的。有可能的话,还可以生成新的身份认同或拓展原有的文化观念。

When we suffer from cultural discomfort, we can do more than just remain distant from it. From what has been said above, we can have a rudimentary knowledge of intercultural competence and why we need to sharpen our skills in this field. When people go abroad to travel, study or work, or when they communicate, cooperate, or negotiate in a multicultural environment at home, they may feel delighted and excited. In the same time, they may also feel frustrated, irritated, perplexed, misunderstood or annoyed. It is even possible for them to get into an argument, a conflict or a lawsuit.

Intercultural conflict refers to the perceived or actual incompatibility of values, norms, processes, or goals between a minimum of two cultural parties over content, identity, relational and procedural issues (Ting-Toomey, 2007:194).

When we are in a situation of intercultural conflicts, is there anything we can do other than tolerate passively or just walk away? Can we go further when we communicate with people with different cultural values? Can we find a solution to our dispute? Don't say NO too easily. In many circumstances, we can solve the problem to various extents by learning the rudimentary knowledge and practicing skills of intercultural competence.

When we are confronted with cultural discomfort, we can do more than just keep the surface harmony or turn to attack. Some people think that they are easy-going and gentle. They always avoid confrontation with others. Intercultural competence is something they will never make use of. In fact, a lack of awareness and the skills of intercultural competence affects our words and deeds in many aspects. We may hear such words in our daily life:

"I don't want to have a foreigner as my boyfriend. They look weird."

"East and west, home is the best. I feel the most comfortable at home."

"Your foreign boyfriend won't marry you. He is just leading you on."

"The foreigner asked me whether we have red-light district in our city the moment he arrived at the hotel (with a contemptuous look)."

Are you aware that the negative feelings listed above result from many factors? You will learn about these factors in a profound way by reading this book and getting involved in the interactive exercises in it. You will realize that intercultural communication is a process in which the interlocutors need to break through their disposition and values, to break the blocks of internal psychology and external power. Then they will be able to construct new knowledge and seek solutions to their problems.

We don't naturally acquire intercultural competence and the ability to communicate effectively and comfortably with the people in a culture when we have learned only the knowledge about their culture. We have learned a lot of cultural knowledge about other countries or nationalities, such as American culture, which is the most familiar to us. But why do so many of our friends or children still feel anxious or have frictions with others after they go to America? We should be aware that knowledge of a certain culture does not automatically give us the ability to communicate effectively and comfortably with individuals in that culture. This is because a specific communication involves a specific context—the understanding of the "specific" values of "specific" parties/groups and their "specific" identities, "specific" environment and "specific" mentality and mood. The key to developing intercultural competence is exploring these "specific" factors and how to make use of and synchronize them.

We may create and apply intercultural strategies which suit the contexts after weighing the advantages and disadvantages. It is natural that sometimes we give up our initial intentions to break the intercultural barrier for various reasons. It would be blind to encourage people to break through their old values and dispositions without considering the circumstances. On the contrary, we encourage people to cultivate intercultural awareness and adapt themselves in order to reduce their discomfort. It would be already fantastic if people were able to find a little different perspective or a little better solution under certain circumstances.

Therefore, if we want to enhance intercultural competence, in addition to the knowledge of a culture, we need to understand what exactly happens in an intercultural communication process. We need to master some skills to get into the process smoothly and to adjust all kinds of factors to get the most of communicative goal. We can even mediate our identities or expand our cultural horizons.

思考 & 讨论 Reflection and discussion

1. 一个人的跨文化能力和他的个人价值观之间有什么样的关系呢？
2. 你是性格内向的人吗？当你累了烦了不愿意去更多地了解对方或跟对方交流时，是不是就意味着你的跨文化能力就很弱呢？
3. 你怎样理解"最好不要得罪领导"这种交流心态？

1. What's the relationship between intercultural competence and personal values?
2. Are you an introverted person? Are you unwilling to learn about or communicate with others when you are tired or annoyed? Does this mean that you are weak in intercultural competence?
3. How do you view that "one had better not offend his/her superiors or bosses?"

学习者自己的提问和反思 Your own questions and reflections

1. _____

2. _____
   _____

第一节 什么是跨文化能力？我们为什么要培养它？
Theme 1 Development of intercultural competence

3. _____

互动小锦囊 Toolkits for interaction

2006年，美国学者Deardorff对学者和教育行政人员"怎样理解跨文化能力的构成因素"做了一个调查。根据调查结果，她勾勒出一个可视化的图表，展现了认可度较高的三个方面的因素（"必要的态度"、"知识和理解"、"技能"）以及掌握它们后期待达到的内部和外部效果。（Deardorff，2006:254）这个调查活动及其结论受到比较广泛的关注。

跨文化能力"金字塔"图表

期待的外部效果：
(基于自己的跨文化的知识、技能和态度)进行有效、得体的行动和沟通，并在某种程度上达成自己的目标

期待的内部效果：
文化参照体系或价值判断视角的调整：
适应性(适应不同的沟通风格和行为/适应新的文化环境)；
灵活性(选择并应用适宜的沟通风格和行为/认知的灵活性)；
民族相对主义观点；
移情

知识和理解：
文化自觉；
对文化的深入理解和学习(包括文化语境、文化的作用和影响力以及他人对世界的看法)；
特定的文化信息；
社会语言意识

技能：
聆听、观察、诠释
分析、评估、联系

必要的态度：
尊重（尊重其它的文化和文化多样性）；
开放（对跨文化学习和与来自其它文化的人交往持开放态度；延迟判断）；
好奇心和积极探索（容忍模糊性和不确定性）

In 2006, the American scholar, Darla K. Deardorff, conducted a survey among intercultural scholars and administrators from higher education and one of the goals is to identify elements of intercultural competence. According to the research results, she sketched a chart showing some of the more accepted factors (in three aspects: "requisite attitudes", "knowledge and comprehension" and "skills") and the desired internal and external outcomes if those factors are attained. (Deardorff, 2006:254)

1.2 我们为什么要提高跨文化能力?
Developing your intercultural competence

Pyramid Model of Intercultural Competence

```
DESIRED EXTERNAL OUTCOME:
Behaving and communicating effectively and
appropriately (based on one's intercultural
knowledge, skills, and attitudes) to achieve one's
goals to some degree

DESIRED INTERNAL OUTCOME:
Informed frame of reference/fillter shift:
Adaptability (to different communication styles & behaviors;
   adjustment to new cultrual environments);
Flexibility (selecting and using appropriate communication
   styles and behaviors; cognitive flexibility);
Ethnorelative view;
Empathy

Knowledge & Comprehension:          ⟷      Skills:
Cultural self-awareness;                   To listen, observe, and interpret
Deep understanding and knowledge of        To analyze, evaluate, and relate
   culture (including contexts, role
   and impact of culture & others'
   world views);
Culture-specific information;
Sociolinguistic awareness

Requisite Attitudes:
Respect (valuing other cultures, cultural diversity);
Openness (to intercultural learning and to people from other cultures, withholding judgment);
Curiosity and discovery (tolerating ambiguity and uncertainty)
```

 互动&体验 Interaction

1. 你可能跟某一个人为某件事情产生过争执和矛盾。那件事情至今有没有得到解决?你觉得发生不快的原因可能是什么呢?按照上图中的"跨文化能力'金字塔'图表",你觉得是哪些因素导致你们发生争执的?

2. 上文展示的"跨文化能力'金字塔'图表"中,跨文化交流构成因素是通过"态度+知识+技能"的逻辑思路完成的。我们可以考虑通过"时间+空间"的逻辑思路,对一个跨文化交流过程的各个构成因素,如开放、尊重、保持好奇心、学习和探索文化知识、保持同理心、有效沟通、延迟判断等等,来重新排列组合一下:

3. 跨文化交流过程中,交流者当时的心态和情绪非常关键。一个和谐的交流过程的实现,有时需要放松的心态、平和的情绪、好奇心和积极的交流动机。读一读下面的文字,你可以安全地遵循原来的想法,也可以静下心来,尝试体验下情绪和想法的转化。

第一节 什么是跨文化能力？我们为什么要培养它？
Theme 1　Development of intercultural competence

烦你！不想跟你讲话！	-»»»	现在我情绪太激动，给我半天时间，晚上跟你谈。
男女共浴?！OMG！太龌龊了！	-»»»	我们去体验下，看看到底是什么样子的。
出国旅行太累太麻烦，我还是在家追追剧，打打牌吧！	-»»»	听说那个邮轮上面的自助餐连吃三天，顿顿不重样，花样多得不得了啊～吃货如我，要不报名试试？
中国的面包做得太甜太松，根本不能叫面包。我还是尽量多买点自己适口的面包带在路上。	-»»»	这家中国的面包店看上去不错，进去看看，说不定里面有我喜欢吃的。
北方人喝酒太猛太野蛮，不跟他们喝。	-»»»	今天被他们多灌了两杯，感觉也不错嘛！

1. You have probably been at odds with someone for something. Have you solved the problem? What do you think is the cause of your dispute? According to the *Pyramid Model of Intercultural Competence* above, which factors led to your dispute?

2. The *Pyramid Model of Intercultural Competence* is arranged along the logical line of "attitude+knowledge+skills" during the process of an intercultural communication. We may try to rearrange those components, for example, openness, curiosity, empathy, respect, delaying judgment, effectiveness of communication, etc., with the logical line of "time sequence+ space sequence":

3. Attitudes and moods of the participants play an important role in the process of intercultural communication. Good communication requires a relaxed, peaceful mood, curiosity and a positive attitude. Read the following examples. You can follow your heart or you can try to settle down to think about it in a different way. Let's try to feel the change of moods and thoughts in the following examples.

I'm mad at you! Don't talk to me now!	- »»»	I'm in a bad mood now. Give me half a day to calm down. I will talk to you in the evening.
Men and women bathe in the same pool! OMG! That is disgusting!	- »»»	Let's go and see what it is really like.
Travelling abroad is too tiring and troublesome. I'll just stay at home to watch some soaps and play cards.	- »»»	I heard that the buffet in that passenger liner is so varied that you don't get the same food for three days. It's awesome for a foodie like me. I have to sign up for it.
Chinese bread is too sweet and soft. It's no bread at all. I will buy some palatable bread and take it with me.	- »»»	This Chinese bakery looks nice. I should go in and check whether they have something else that I like.
Northern Chinese are heavy drinkers. I would rather not drink with them.	- »»»	I was forced to drink two shots by them. It's not that terrible!

援引阅读 Quoted readings

"子曰:'知变化之道者,其知神之所为乎? 易有圣人之道四焉:以言者尚其辞,以动者尚其变,以制器者尚其象,以卜筮者尚其占。'

是以君子将有为也,将有行也,问焉而以言。其受命如是响,无有远近幽深,遂知来物。非天下之至精,其孰能与于此? 参吾以变,错综其数,通其变,遂成天地之文;极其数,遂定天下之象。非天下之至变,其孰能与于此? 易无思也,无为也,寂然不动,感而遂通天下之故。非天下之至神,其孰能与于此?"

——黄寿祺,周善文.《周易译注》.上海:上海古籍出版社,2010 年.

"Intercultural scholars and higher education administrators did not define intercultural competence in relation to specific components (i. e., what specifically constitutes intercultural knowledge, skills, and attitudes). Instead, both groups preferred definitions that were broader in nature. Although this may be a surprising conclusion, this is actually in keeping with the literature in that most definitions are more general. However, it is important to note that a key criticism of existing definitions is that they are either too general or provide a disjointed list of attributes." (p.253)

—Deardorff, D. K. (2006). Identification and assessment of intercultural competence as a student outcome of internalization. *Journal of Studies in International Education*, 10(3), 241–266.

"IC is conceived here as an integral whole of cognitive, affective and behavioral factors that influence the understanding of, and interaction with, diversity in a broad sense, and which can be developed through education and/or experience. This definition considers recent developments in IC studies in the fields of both language education and intercultural communication, where a relationship is increasingly envisaged between intercultural competence and communication on the one hand, and postmodern discourses about the notion of multiple, hybrid, fluid identities on the other. Intercultural competence is thus linked to how individuals socially position themselves in interactions (e.g., according to their nationally, genre, age, social status, etc.), to their awareness of such positioning, and to their willingness and ability to recognise and negotiate the others' multiple identities as much as their own."

—Borghetti, C. (2017). Is there really a need for assessing intercultural competence? Some ethical issues. *Journal for Intercultural Communication*, 44. http://immi.se/intercultural/nr44/borghetti.html

"但是人们也已经指出,这种被勉强构造起来的不可能性,又自相矛盾,又被经验为

第一节 什么是跨文化能力？我们为什么要培养它？
Theme 1　Development of intercultural competence

一种不可能的可能性。这种不可能性为了成其为不可能性，在其本质中又隐含着这样一回事情：此现在不可能与之共存的另外一个现在，以某种方式也是一个相同者，也是一个作为现在的现在，并与那不可能与它共存的现在共存的不可能性只有从某种共存出发、从某种非-同时的（non-simultane）同时性（simultaneite）出发才能被如此这般地设定。在这种非同时性的同时性中，现在的他异性与同一性被维系于某个同一者的被区分了的因素中。用拉丁语说，cum 或共-存的共（co-）只有其不可能性出发才有意义，反之亦然。不可能（两个现在的共存）只能显现在一种综合中，（综合这个词是中性的：它并不意味着设定、主动性、施动者），让我们说：显现在某种共谋性（complicite）或共-牵连（/共同隐含：co-implication）中，这种共谋性或共牵连把若干实际的现在（他们分别被说成是过去和将来）维系（maintenant）在一起。对若干当前的现在的不可能的维持，作为对若干当前现在的维持是可能的。时间就是这种不可能的可能性的名字。"（第205页）

——雅克·德里达著.《解构与思想的未来》.夏可君编校.吉林：吉林人民出版社，2006 年.

第二节
松动身心,意识到自己正进入"跨文化通道"

Theme 2
Looseness and the awareness of the "intercultural tunnel"

第二节 松动身心,意识到自己正进入"跨文化通道"
Theme 2　Looseness and the awareness of the " intercultural tunnel"

2.1　让身心松动
Loosening up

 理论引介 Introduction

虽然一个文化的边界地带是动态的,但一定的边界始终是存在的,因为人们需要文化身份的认同,而文化的边界可以基本上将一个文化身份与另一个文化身份区分开来。所以,从边界打开一个缝隙,让其它的文化观念能够渗入,甚至最后逐渐丰润其中心区域,有时是非常困难的事情。就像 Rickles 在为著名的物理学家 Bohm 晚年的著作《论对话》(*On Dialogue*)(2014)写的前言中所说的那样:"玻姆式对话需要努力——它是一个积极进取的过程,它需要类似于佛教所说的某种程度的自我否认,也需要在某种程度上对本我的消灭。"

虽然我们不能也不应该随意地调整一个稳定的文化观念,但我们是不是可以达成一个共识,就是在主动或被动地选择进入一个"跨文化通道"时,如果我们能根据实际情况适当地调整和丰润我们的文化观念,会有助于有效舒适地交流。而调整和丰润本身意味着一种变化,要变化,那首先就是自己变得柔软,提供产生变化需要的缺口。因此,让我们的身心变得柔软是第一位的,也就是说,我们在精神上先要有一个松弛的状态。

放松是东方古老智慧中的一个重要内容,在印度瑜伽哲学、中国的道家修行方式比如太极拳中,都是重要的训练内容。中国太极拳大师杨禹廷、吴图南、汪永泉等都是松柔艺术大家。太极拳大家都论述过太极拳的"松功",认为"松功是太极拳练家终身追求,一世修炼的最高境界的功法。"(祝大彤:2005)"松者,蓬松也;宽而不紧;轻松也;放开也,轻松畅快也;不坚凝也;含有小孔以容其它物质之特性也。"(吴图南:2013-4)

这种松动的意识和状态,可以贯穿地运用到跨文化交流的各个阶段——一旦当我们心理上感受到任何负面的感觉如"不同"、"不舒服"、"别扭"、"委屈"、"惊悚"、"荒谬"、"愤怒"、"痛苦"时,训练自己下意识地采取一种"不对抗"的态度,静下心来,感受各种"阻滞"的位置、程度、原因,准备一个开放对话的心态,这样能进一步获得更多的时间和空间去学习,给自己机会去看到、听到、接触到新的信息,然后去对比、反观,进一步理解不熟悉的观念,或调整自己原有的观念,最终获得力量,打通阻滞,感知正确的应对方案去顺势化解,而不是被情绪控制,失去正确思考和判断的能力,让事情变得更加复杂和失控,更不是"安全地"、"忠实地"僵化固守原则,封闭自己,不去了解和学习。因为任何一个文化观念,都只是在特定环境中形成的特定思维,如果固守一个文化观念,当它在与另一个特定环境中另一个特定思维发生碰撞时,往往起到阻碍交流的作用。

　　松动练习给我们一个良好的心理环境,从而准备了开放的态度,去尽量积极参与跨文化交流,比较有效地通过"跨文化通道"。在一份调查报告(Van Maele, Vassilicos, & Borghetti: 2016)里很多被调查者对"开放"给出了很多自己的理解,包括更多理解和接受、扩展视野、不要过多预设和期待、勇于尝试各种新鲜事物、更多时候说"同意""好的",等等。

Although the border area of a culture is hybrid and dynamic, the border itself is still there, because a border separates the cultural identities that each group needs for themselves. Therefore it seems almost impossible to open a seam to let another cultural value permeate even a little. As understood by Dean Rickles (2014), who wrote the foreword to *On Dialogue* by David Bohm, the well-known theoretical physicist, "Bohmian dialogue requires *effort* - it is an active procedure, demanding a level of self-denial and ego elimination akin to Buddhism."

Although we cannot adjust a relatively stable cultural value at will, we may finally reach a consensus that when we actively or passively enter the " intercultural tunnel", it contributes to a more comfortable and productive communication if we can adjust our own cultural values a little bit under different contexts. Yet to adjust, means to be willing to make a change. And to make a change may mean making your mind "loosened up" so that your thought can turn and move. Consequently, to make our mind a little "loose and relaxed" is of prime importance, and this means that we have to be mentally relaxed.

"Looseness in body and mind" is an important part of the ancient oriental wisdom. It is highly emphasized in Indian Yoga philosophy or Chinese philosophies, for example, in Taoist Taichi practice. Chinese Taichi masters Yang Yuting, Wu Tunan, Wang Yongquan and some others are experts in looseness and relaxation exercise. Masters of Taichi believe that "looseness is the lifelong quest and the only way to the highest state of Taichi practioners." (Zhu: 2005) "Being loose means being broad, relaxed, open, carefree, light, smooth, and with small holes to hold other substances." (Wu, 2013 - 4)

To apply the concept of looseness to intercultural competence practice, we need to train ourselves to readily adopt a non-resistant attitude that breaks down the counter force. That is, when we have negative feelings such as discomfort, awkwardness, injustice, panic, absurdity, anger or agony, we should firstly calm down to figure out the position, degree and cause of such "blocks" and then rest ourselves to gain more time and room to learn. We see, hear, and discover new knowledge, and then compare with and reflect on our own feelings. Then we may be able to further understand the unfamiliar ideas or adjust what we insist in a new context. With the newly gained insight, hopefully we will be able to break the block and find a solution. If we "naturally", "loyally", and "safely" stick to our original thinking, we will always be overwhelmed by negative feelings and lose the ability to see the overall situation, which will make the situation more complicated, and the situation may even get out of control. We then realize that any cultural understanding is often limited in a new context. There is no "universal" cultural understanding that is accepted in every corner of the world.

Looseness and relaxation prepare us for a more open attitude to enter an "intercultural tunnel". In a survey report (Van Maele, Vassilicos, & Borghetti: 2016), many informants give their own understandings of "openness", such as more understanding and more acceptance, widening horizons, less presumptions and anticipations, being braver to try new things, saying more "yes" and "good" more often.

思考 & 讨论 Reflection and discussion

1. 你曾经的"底线"或"原则"在哪些情况下主动或被动地发生改变过？改变时你的感觉如何呢？

2. 曾经的价值观发生了变化，是件可耻的事吗？

3. "放松"的对立面"紧张"和"僵硬"会给跨文化交流带来怎样的负面影响？

1. Under what circumstances did you actively or passively go beyond your bottom line or go against your principles? How did you feel then?

2. Is it a shame or a betrayal to adjust your values?

3. What negative influence do "tension" and "rigidity", the opposite of looseness, bring to intercultural communication?

学习者自己的提问和反思 Your own questions and reflections

1. _____

_____

2. _____

3. _____

互动小锦囊 Toolkits for interaction

太极拳放松的基本规律

"松中生运动"是道家哲学原理"无极生太极、太极生阴阳"在具体生活中的体现。张志明先生(2017)总结了五条太极拳放松的基本规律,归纳如下:

1. 虚极静笃松:感受身体各个部位和细小的空间之间拉开了距离,相互之间没有妨碍,各得其所,身体内外均匀普遍地放松。

2. 偏沉则随松:顺着身体和引力之间的关系,借力发力,将身体自身重量所包含的位能转化成动能,不求运动而自然释放出能量,像风因松而生风,水因松而流动一样。

3. 阴阳对称松:对身体前后、左右、上下有阴阳相对的概念,每个运动单元都需要"阴松"和"阳松"的结合,能量才能有收有放。

4. 点线面体松:所有的放松过程都是从点到线到面到体的过程,浑然一体,全身舒展,畅快内心。

5. 有意无意松:模糊、宏观地用意,解放自己,才能出现真意,能量才能畅达。

Some principles of Taichi looseness practice

" Movements originate from looseness" is the application in practice of the fundamental Taoist philosophy of "Wuji generates Taiji, and Taiji generates two complementary forces (Yi and Yang)". Zhang (2017) summarizes the five principles of Taichi Looseness as follows:

1. Looseness from stillness and stableness: to relax in stillness to feel that every small part of the body has stretched apart from the others and positioned itself well without mutual intrusion.

2. Looseness from following the body weight: to relax and learn to take the advantage of gravity to transfer the static and potential energy in a part of the body into kinetic energy. This is to generate energy from stillness and emptiness, like currents of air and water.

3. Looseness of both Yin and Yang: to bear in mind that Yin and Ying always go along with each other in front and back parts of the body, the left and right sides of the body, the upper and lower parts of the body. Every movement should involve both Yin and Yang so

that the energy can stretch out and withdraw smoothly.

4. Looseness from an overall process: to always relax in a process from a dot, to a line, to an area and then to a three-dimensional space. Then the whole body is relaxed and light.

5. Looseness between consciousness and unconsciousness: to relax and fall into a space somewhere between consciousness and unconsciousness so that energy can be guided and directed to arrive at the place where you want it to be.

 互动&体验 Interaction

1. 找一个安静的地方，坐下或平躺。按照下面的步骤练习：
（1）慢慢感受自己的心跳，一直到它平静下来。
（2）放松自己的眉头。（如果感觉放松了，说明原来它的是紧的）。
（3）放松自己的后颈。（如果感觉放松了，说明原来它的是紧的）。
（4）放松自己的肩膀。（如果感觉放松了，说明原来它的是紧的）。
（5）放松自己的腰部。（如果感觉放松了，说明原来它的是紧的）。
（6）放松自己的每一个脚趾。（如果感觉放松了，说明原来它的是紧的）。

2. 我们来做一个好玩的游戏。
（1）找一个你认识或不认识的人。
（2）找一个不大的空地。
（3）用你的某一个手指尖和对方的某一个手指尖触碰在一起。
（4）在一直保持指尖触碰的情况下，你们各自做各种自己喜欢做的动作。
（5）你们身体其它部分不用触碰在一起，但碰在一起也可以，也可以一起说说话，或用眼睛看对方的各种动作。
（6）看看你们的指尖保持触碰的时间有多久。

3. 下面这些原则，你可以坚持，也可以尝试放松下来，用新的视角重新观照。例一已经给出。

你的原则	稍微开放些的观点	更加开放些的观点
1. 我是个素食者。吃荤的人是没有修养，没有环保意识的。	我在吃荤的人面前不批评不反对，不想要去改变他们，但我想知道他们为什么要吃荤。	吃荤的人可能是他们身体的需要，也是他们热爱美食、热爱生活的表现吧。
2		
3		
4		
5		

1. Find a quiet place and then sit down or lie down. Do as follows:

i. Feel your heartbeat until it becomes regular and slow.

ii. Relax your eyebrow. (If you feel it loosening now, it means that it was tight.)

iii. Relax your neck. (If you feel it loosing now, it means that it was tight.)

iv. Relax your shoulder. (If you feel it loosing now, it means that it was tight.)

v. Relax your waist. (If you feel it loosing now, it means that it was tight.)

vi. Relax each of your toes, one at a time. (If you feel them loosing now, it means that they were tight.)

2. Let's play an interesting game.

i. Invite a friend or a stranger to join.

ii. Find a place.

iii. Stretch out your hand to lay one of your fingers on any one finger of your game partner.

iv. Keep the two fingers always together and then do whatever you two want. You can talk with each other or watch each other's movements, with or without other parts of your bodies contacting.

v. See how long the two fingers can stay in contact.

3. You can safely stick to the following principles as before, but you can also try to adjust them with an open mind. The first example has been given.

Your principles	Adjustment with an open mind	Adjustment with an even more open mind
1. I am a vegetarian. People who eat meat are uncivilized and not environment-friendly.	When I see people eat meat, I do not criticize them and start to wonder why they do so.	Some people eat meat because their bodies need it. It also shows their love for food and life. They may have different understandings of eating meat.
2.		
3.		
4.		
5.		

第二节　松动身心，意识到自己正进入"跨文化通道"
Theme 2　Looseness and the awareness of the "intercultural tunnel"

2.2　意识到自己正在进入"跨文化通道"
Being aware of the "intercultural tunnel"

理论引介 Introduction

很久以来，跨文化能力培养大多数时候停留在理论阐述层面，而对于一个主动或被动地进入跨文化交流的个体来说，这是一个实实在在的体验过程。当他进入跨文化交流的当口，他有可能是兴奋、愉快、顺利的，也可能会出现深深不解，感到奇怪、荒谬、委屈等各种情绪。我们除了先放松之外，可能要马上想到，这个情绪的来源，不一定是简单的道德观念冲突、权力失衡产生的冲突或性格的冲突，而是我可能进入了某个"跨文化通道"，我可能要用全新的心态、智慧、技巧去应对一个新的局面。否则，我们永远会延续以前的老做法，要不简单地贴上标签，要不逆来顺受，要不能躲则躲，失去一个新的沟通或学习的机会，不能达成期待的交流目的。

学者们曾用 intercultural encounter（霍尔，2011；Byram 等，2010；Van Maele & Mertens, 2014), intercultural experience（霍尔，2011），a series of sustained encounters, process of intercultural engagement (Holmes, 2012)等英文短语来定义这个实际操作层面的过程。学者 Kramsch (1998) 认为这个跨文化交流过程是"一个场域(place)"，在这

个"场域"中，人们遇到了不同的文化和世界观，并通过协商来调适原有的文化身份、社会身份和文化表达形式。"Holmes"多次使用"location"（场所）、"process"（过程）等词汇来描述并强调它的时间和空间特征。她认为一个交流者的跨文化能力在这个过程中是最容易被观察到的。(2012, 708 - 710)

从实用操作角度出发，我们不妨用"跨文化通道"(intercultural tunnel)来描述这个过程。我们认为，文化现象、文化身份、文化行为等，背后都是文化观念在支撑。所以，围绕两个相互碰撞的文化观念所进行的交流，可以形成一个特定的"跨文化通道"：它是在某个特定时间段和某个特定空间里针对某个话题（两个相碰撞的文化观念）进行的两

人或多人交流，并最终达成/未达成某种交流目的；或者是针对某个特定话题（文化观念）在不同时间段和不同空间延绵数次的交碰，并相对来说达成/未达成某种交流目的。我们可以发现，这个"跨文化通道"具有以下一些特性：

首先，"跨文化通道"是一个人（通过者）所载有的文化观念与另一个不同文化观念的交碰过程，因此这个通过者不一定仅和另一个人交流，可能是跟更多人的交流，这个人也不一定是非要进入一个国家或一个新的语言环境，只要两个不同的文化观念发生碰撞，他就进入了"跨文化通道"。

第二，"跨文化通道"里某个文化观念和另一个文化观念发生的接触、对话、调适等行为，具有线性的时间性，虽然不同行为发生时间可能会有重叠，但仍然有个基本的时间先后顺序。从一个文化观念载有者的行为角度来描述，这个时间过程是这样的：

相遇→松动→延迟判断→搜集信息→共情尊重→协商→调整边界→反哺丰润

第三，在空间上，进入"跨文化通道"并不是仅仅进入一个新的地理环境或语言环境，而更多的时候是进入了一个"文化观念交汇空间"。这个空间可能是短时间内某个地方，也可能在数日、数月、数年中不同的地方，当某两个文化观念的碰撞和调适相对完成，达到一定的交际目的，或"通过者"放弃交流，撤退回原位，这个"跨文化通道"就不再活跃。

第四，"跨文化通道"并不是一个压抑的、与外界隔绝的空间，而是立体的，与外界融通的。人们会在一开始感受到种种不舒适，得不到外界的帮助，但如果掌握调节技巧，学会与外界沟通，最后就会成功"走出通道"。相反，则撤退出这个通道，没有达成交流目的。

最后，我们认为，跨文化通道在时间和空间上是具有开放性的。通道在开端是开放的，交流者有时是被动地进入，有时是主动地、有意识地进入；而由于某个文化对话在某个阶段只是相对地完成了，其中的两个文化观念还可以继续保留对话，因此跨文化通道在出口处也保有开放的姿态，鼓励交流双方在更久远的时间内、更广泛的空间内，继续深入对话。

敏锐地意识到我们作为某个文化观念的载有者进入了一个"跨文化通道"还远远不够。我们还需要意识到，在进入、通过和结束整个"跨文化通道"过程中，我们对自身所带的"文化烙印"和对方所带的"文化烙印"、我们情绪控制、交流动机、态度、交流技能、批判性反思能力等，都会持续地、深深地影响我们在这个时空里的行为和交流结果。

因此，我们最后可能会发现，处理"跨文化通道"里的不适和冲突，原来不一定要采用一些激烈的方式，如语言攻击、肢体冲撞、解除关系、惩罚、制裁、投诉、仲裁等，也不是靠嘲讽、讥笑、鄙视、辱骂来被动地回应，通过这个通道需要独特的认知、处理技巧和解决途径。在后面的章节里，我们会按照一定的时空顺序逐步讨论和体验这些"装备"，了解它们是什么，什么时候该用什么，并且尝试去运用。

第二节　松动身心,意识到自己正进入"跨文化通道"
Theme 2　Looseness and the awareness of the "intercultural tunnel"

For a long time, development of intercultural competence has more or less remained at a theoretical level. However, individuals who experience intercultural communication actively or passively feel it is a very vivid, and practical process. They may first feel excited, amazed, cheerful, puzzled, strange, ridiculous, or wronged. Then apart from relaxing ourselves, we also need to be aware that the negative feelings we have are not necessarily caused by conflicts of moral ideas, imbalanced power or incompatible personalities. Instead, they may result from the fact that you have entered an "intercultural tunnel", where you have different cultural values from those of others, and where you have to respond to various situations with an adjusted attitude, new knowledge and skills. If we continue the old ways of refusing to re-think our position or of labeling people rashly, resigning ourselves to adversities and running away from difficulties, we may lose the opportunity to communicate and learn and we will never be able to experience successful communication.

Scholars use terms like intercultural encounter (Hall, 2011; Byram et al, 2010; Van Maele & Mertens, 2014), intercultural experience (Hall, 2011), a series of sustained encounters, or process of intercultural engagement (Holmes, 2012) to define the practical steps in intercultural communication. Kramsch (1998) thinks that intercultural communication is a "place" where people first meet different cultures and world outlooks and then adjust their old cultural and social identity and cultural expressions. Holmes uses terms like "location" and "process" to describe and emphasize the features of time and space in intercultural communication. She believes that it is in this process that one's intercultural competence is most easily observed. (2012, 708 - 710)

To help those who actually experience the intercultural communication see this process more figuratively, and reduce their frustrations, if any, with operational tools, we can use the term "intercultural tunnel" to describe this process. We realized that different cultural values lie behind various cultural phenomena, cultural norms and cultural behaviors. Hence a certain "intercultural tunnel" is formed throughout the interaction of two cultural values.

An "intercultural tunnel" refers to the process of a person (passer) who communicates with another person or another group of people who have different understanding of a certain cultural phenomenon in a certain time and space. The passer may either manage to, or fail to achieve the communication goal. An "international tunnel" also refers to a long-term communication a person (passer) holds with another person or another group of people who have different cultural values continually in different times and places. An "intercultural tunnel" has the following characteristics:

First of all, the actual conflicting elements in an "intercultural tunnel" are two or more seemingly conflicting cultural values, therefore the "passer" who goes through it will communicate with one or more than one person. He doesn't necessarily go to a foreign country or a new place, or speak a different language to enter an "intercultural tunnel". An "intercultural tunnel" is formed as soon as a person encounters one or more different cultural values on a certain subject.

Secondly, the encounter, exploration, adjustment and other actions taken in the "intercultural tunnel" go along a certain time line. The time of these actions may overlap sometimes but generally they're in chronological order. A passer with a certain cultural value or norm may go through these actions in the following process in an "intercultural tunnel": contact→loosen up→delay judgment→explore→empathize→negotiate→adjust→enrich

Thirdly, in terms of place "intercultural tunnel" refers to not only the new geological and linguistic environment but also any meeting place of conflicting cultural values and norms. It could be a specific place for a one-time communication or several places for a relatively long-term communication spanning several days, months or even years over certain cultural values or norms. The "intercultural tunnel" will be inactive for the time being when the adjustments have been completed and the aim of communication has been achieved, or the passer gives up the intention for communication and retreats to the original ground.

Fourthly, an "intercultural tunnel" is not a sealed, cut-off entity but outward looking and communal. At the very beginning people may feel suffocated and helpless, but with skills learned they may pass through the tunnel and relatively achieve the aim of their communication. Finally, the intercultural tunnel is open on both ends. It opens at the beginning, encouraging the passer to enter with an intercultural awareness and initiatives for communication. Since the dialogue between two cultural values or norms only completes for a certain purpose, the intercultural tunnel also opens on the other end, to encourage the dialogue to continue on a boarder time and space base.

It is far from sufficient to enter an "intercultural tunnel" with a keen sense that we are carriers of certain cultural values and norms. We need to know more than that. A number of factors actually continually and profoundly affect our behaviors and communication in this tunnel, such as the control of emotions, motives for communication, communicative skills, and critical ways of thinking.

Therefore, we may in the end realize that we can actually handle the cultural discomforts and conflicts with better techniques and solutions instead of using fierce ways such as verbal attack, physical clash, termination of relationship, punishment, sanction, complaint or arbitration. It is no good idea to passively react to the discomforts and

第二节 松动身心，意识到自己正进入"跨文化通道"
Theme 2 Looseness and the awareness of the "intercultural tunnel"

conflicts by jeering, mocking, belittling or even cursing. In the following themes, we will talk about the techniques that could help us according to a certain order of time and space. We will find out what they are, when to use them and try to practice them.

思考 & 讨论 Reflection and discussion

1. 根据前面对文化内涵的阐释，是不是人与人之间观念的不同都是文化观念的不同？为什么？
2. 到了一个陌生的地方，如果气候不适，水土不服，是文化因素导致的吗？
3. 在一个不太顺利的跨文化交流过程里，可能会出现哪些不舒服的情绪？

1. Based on the understanding of culture, do you agree or disagree that all the differences between people come from different cultural values? Why?
2. When you get to a strange place, is your disagreement with the climate and place caused by cultural factors?
3. What uncomfortable feelings one may feel in an unfavorable intercultural communication?

学习者自己的提问和反思 Your own questions and reflections

1. _____
   _____
2. _____
   _____
3. _____
   _____

互动小锦囊 Toolkits for interaction

下面这个简单的穿越"跨文化通道"的示意图，可以帮助我们看清实际操作的方法和步骤，并给予我们信心，相信我们因为遇到文化冲突而产生的负面感受，是在很大程度上可以得到缓解的。

The following sketch of "intercultural tunnel" shows us the practical methods and operational steps in intercultural communication. It gives us some confidence because it tells us how to lessen the negative feelings we experience in intercultural conflict.

2.2 意识到自己正在进入"跨文化通道"
Being aware of the "intercultural tunnel"

相遇→松动→延迟判断→搜集信息→共情→协商→调整边界→反哺丰润

contact → lossen up → delay judgment → explore → empathize → negotiate → adjust → enrich

一个相对完成了的"跨文化通道"
A relatively completed "intercultural tunnel"

 互动&体验 Interaction

1. 下面这些情况下,你可以体会进入"跨文化通道"的瞬间。请一边阅读,一边细细感受进入跨文化通道的微妙瞬间中,你的心态变化。

»»»» 你在巴黎旅游时,走进一间卖老唱片的商店。全是外文封面,你和老板语言不通。你不打算说什么,准备自己翻翻唱片就离开。但或者你也可以……

»»»» 你在英国一所大学里闲逛,看到很多大楼上都插着"彩虹旗",你很惊奇这里的"开放",也很受不了他们的"开放"。但或者你也可以……

»»»» 你坐在一家茶馆里,看见一个"老外"正到处问人,有没有牛奶可以加到龙井茶里。你扑哧一笑,偷偷拍下他,发给微信好友:"真是奇葩啊,哈哈哈~",但或者你也可以……

对于上面这些"意识到一个跨文化通道并尝试进入"的过程,你的感觉是?

很棒　　别扭　　为自己骄傲　　发现了自己的潜力　　没有以前来得痛快
没感觉痛苦　　累死了　　不喜欢　　再试试　　恐惧　　忐忑

2. 代沟真的存在吗?无论如何,父母和子女之间总有各种观念不一致的时候,比如,半夜11点半,18岁的女儿的房间里,灯还亮着。你作为母亲/儿女通常怎样做?效果如何?

这也可能是一个母女之间的"跨文化通道"。按照前面的"跨文化通道示意图",你作为母亲/儿女,今后可能会怎么做?

母亲过去的做法	母亲今后可能的做法	女儿过去的做法	女儿今后可能的做法
觉得灯光亮影响睡眠,生气,并且从10点半到11点半N次催促她关灯。		大叫道:"你烦不烦?我这么大了还要你管!"	
大喊大骂女儿不听话,不管父母辛苦一天。		戴上耳机,反锁房门。	

续 表

母亲过去的做法	母亲今后可能的做法	女儿过去的做法	女儿今后可能的做法
用备用钥匙开女儿房门，关掉女儿房间的灯。		大发雷霆，觉得个人隐私受到极大侮辱。警告父母如果再这样，就搬出去住。	
看见女儿正在手机上玩游戏，气得把她手机夺过来砸在地上。		直接泪奔，大哭，冲出家门。	

3. 下面这些事件中，可能并不是别人为难你或没有修养，而只是文化观念在发生碰撞。我们可以找找有哪些因素会妨碍人们顺利的交流，以达成交流目的。更为关键的是，我们可以讨论一下，这些因素，在哪些条件下，是可以克服的。

事件 1：留学生导师因为我没有参加课堂讨论，所以给了我差评。我得去跟导师解释，看看能不能改变他的评语，这可是会影响我挂科的。

相碰撞的文化观念：_____

阻碍达到交流目的因素：_____

条件讨论：_____

事件 2：宿舍里有个外国女生，每次我听"中国好声音"，她都把我的偶像歌手批得一塌糊涂，说他们惺惺作态，好"假"，服装也特难看。

相碰撞的文化观念：_____

阻碍达到交流目的因素：_____

条件讨论：_____

事件 3：公司里有个外国同事，总是到处宣扬针灸是害人命的玩意儿。我觉得我应该好好跟同事们解释下针灸是怎么回事，不能让他这么黑我们的中医技术。

相碰撞的文化观念：_____

阻碍达到交流目的因素：_____

2.2 意识到自己正在进入"跨文化通道"
Being aware of the "intercultural tunnel"

条件讨论：_____

_____

事件4：我在欧洲国际机场过安检时，只有我一个人的所有私人物品都被要求拿出来接受检查，我觉得受到了莫大的侮辱。我要去投诉他们这种针对某个人、不顾个人隐私的做法。

相碰撞的文化观念：_____

_____

阻碍达到交流目的因素：_____

_____

条件讨论：_____

_____

1. In the following examples, you will enter an "intercultural tunnel". Please read carefully and feel the subtle changes in your attitudes and behaviors.

»»»» When you are travelling in Paris, you go into a shop that sells old records. The words on the cover are foreign to you. You don't speak the same language as the shop owner. So you intend to leaf through the records and then leave without talking with the shop owner.

Or you can ...

»»»» You are idling about in an English university today. You see many buildings with "rainbow flags" (symbol of homosexualities). You are surprised with their openly supportive attitude to homosexuality and it makes you uncomfortable.

Or you can ...

»»»» You are sitting in a tea house and see a foreigner asking around whether there is milk to add into his Longjing tea. You find it so funny that you take a picture of this and post it in your WeChat circle, saying "What a weirdo!"

Or you can ...

In the above mentioned cases, when you realize that it is an "intercultural tunnel" that you are about to enter, how do you feel?

awesome, awkward, proud, afraid, disturbed, painful, tired, "I have seen my potential." "Not as resolved as before.", "No special feeling.", "I don't like it.", "I will try again.", "It's so tiring."
……

2. Is generation gap a real thing? Anyway, parents and children do disagree on some

第二节 松动身心，意识到自己正进入"跨文化通道"
Theme 2 Looseness and the awareness of the "intercultural tunnel"

things. For example, at 00:30 a.m. the light is still on in an eighteen-year-old daughter's room. There could possibly be an "intercultural tunnel" in this moment between them. What could you they do respectively in the future?

The mother used to do in this way:	The mother could do this in the future:	The daughter used to do in this way:	The daughter could do this in the future:
She feels that the light affected her daughter's sleep and was mad at her. She has been pressing her to turn off the light countless times from 10 p.m.		She cries out, "You are so annoying! I am old enough to take care of my own business."	
She yells at her daughter for not listening to her, saying that she is inconsiderate.		She puts on the headphone and locks the door from inside.	
She opens her daughter's room with a spare key and turns off the light.		She flies into a rage because she thinks her mother has trespassed on her privacy. She warns her mother if she doesn't stop doing this she will move out.	
When she sees her daughter playing games on her smart phone, she gets so angry that she grabs the phone and smacks it onto the floor.		She loses control of her feelings and rushes out of the house with tears running down her face.	

3. When we enter a relatively complete "intercultural tunnel", we actually experience two different cultural values or norms. From the following examples, we may tell that sometimes we run into trouble not because someone intentionally embarrasses us or he/she is rude. It's just the result of different cultural values or norms conflicting with each other. We can try to find the factors that block or promote communication. More importantly, we may discuss in what circumstances we can get over the unfavourable factors.

Case 1: An instructor gave me, an international student, poor marks because I often kept silent in class discussion. I need to talk with him to see if I can change his marks. I may get a D if I allow him to continue doing this.

Conflicting cultural values or norms: _____

_____

Factors that block communication: _____

_____

2.2 意识到自己正在进入"跨文化通道"
Being aware of the "intercultural tunnel"

How to get over it?
_____
_____

Case 2: I have a roommate who is a foreigner. Every time I watch the show "Voice of China", she will say something bad about my idols, saying that they are very pretentious and their clothes look ugly.

Conflicting cultural values or norms: _____
_____

Factors that block communication: _____
_____

How to get over it?
_____

Case 3: I have a foreign colleague who keeps telling people that Chinese acupuncture is harmful and it even kills people. I think it necessary to explain to my other colleagues what acupuncture is really about. I can't just do nothing about his demeaning attitudes towards Chinese medicine.

Acupuncture!

Conflicting cultural values or norms: _____
_____

Factors that block communication: _____
_____

How to get over it?
_____

Case 4: I come from America. Once when I went through the security check at a Chinese railway station, I was the only person who was asked to take out all the personal stuff to be checked. I found that was too insulting. I wanted to lodge a complaint on their singling me out and disregarding personal privacy.

Conflicting cultural values or norms: _____
_____

Factors that block communication: _____
_____

How to get over it?
_____

第二节 松动身心,意识到自己正进入"跨文化通道"
Theme 2 Looseness and the awareness of the "intercultural tunnel"

 援引阅读 Quoted readings

"(太极拳)习练者周身空松,从里到外均一一放松,等于打开了'精灵'进入人体的通道,太极拳'精灵'顺利进入体内,人体得到了太极内功。相反如用力将周身通道堵塞,则太极内功难以进入……太极拳与其它拳种不同,从学练的第一步就要进入松柔功夫的习练。练拳和松柔功夫不能脱节,如果脱节,久而久之,动作僵滞,身上松不下来。"(第42页)

——祝大彤.《太极无处不放松》.《精武》.2005年第10期,42页.

"松与紧是对立统一的。何时松,何时紧,以及放松程度如何,都应做到心中有数。然后持目的而用意导形。对于紧而松,一味放松而不紧,或松软无力,都是错误的。紧而不松,劲合不住,动作僵硬,停滞呆板,呼吸不自然。胸闷,肌肉紧张和涣散,内气不畅,肤感不灵等现象,一味放松,爆发力难生,丢失划圆出方打刚劲的功能。松过了,就不能将劲合住,会出现软塌无力,既无防守能力,也更无进攻之能。整体松不好,会影响练拳功夫的进程。"(第61—62页)

——张迎忠.《谈太极拳松功的作用与训练》.《搏击》.2007年12期,61—62页.

"When our attitudes towards host nationals are rigid and divisive (e.g., ethnocentrism, prejudice, racism, authoritarianism, sexism, ageism, dogmatism, social dominance orientation, closed-mindfulness, etc.), we tend to be intolerant of host nationals' viewpoints. [...] When we have rigid attitudes and have negative expectations we do not look for new information about the host nationals with whom we interact. The more rigid our attitudes, therefore, the lower our ability to predict host nationals' behaviour accurately." (p.432)

——Gudykunst, W. B. (2014, b). An Anxiety/uncertainty management (AUM) theory of strangers' intercultural adjustment. In Gudykunst, W. B. (Ed.), *Theorizing About Intercultural Communication* (pp.419 – 457). Shanghai: Shanghai Foreign Language Education Press.

"Chen and Starosta (1998) also reported some of the first impressions the Japanese visitors had of US Americans. They include that Americans walk very fast, are always in a hurry, always try to talk everything out, and don't respect teachers in school. In this level we tend to understand a culture or its people by the most visible characteristics it possesses. We then apply part of these characteristics to the whole group. For example, Asian students with a high GPA in American colleges are often incorrectly considered as science and math majors because from media we know that Asian students often do better in those areas. Finally, we give the same treatment to each member of the group by saying, for example,

'You are a Japanese, you must be smart.'" (pp.31－32)

——Chen, G. M., & Starosta, W. J. (1998－9). A review of the concept of intercultural awareness. *Human Communication*, 2, 27－54.

"(...) After all, it is easy for each one of us to see that other people are 'blocked' about certain questions, so that without being aware of it, they are avoiding the confrontation of contradictions in certain ideas that may be extremely dear to them.

The very nature of such a 'block' is, however, that it is a kind of insensitivity or 'anesthesia' about one's own contradictions. Evidently then, what is crucial is to be aware of the nature of one's own 'blocks'. If one is alert and attentive, he can see for example that whenever certain questions arise, there are fleeting sensations of fear, which push him away from consideration of these questions, and of pleasure, which attract his thoughts and cause them to be occupied with other questions. So one is able to keep away from whatever it is that he thinks may disturb him. And as a result, he can be subtly defending his own ideas, when he supposes that he is really listening to what other people have to say." (p.5)

——Bohm, D. (2014). *On Dialogue*. New York: Routledge.

第三节
利用概括性知识,同时打破固化刻板的思维

Theme 3
Generalization and non-essentialist perspectives

第三节 利用概括性知识，同时打破固化刻板的思维
Theme 3 Generalization and non-essentialist perspectives

3.1 概括性知识的利用和慎用
Generalizing and over-generalizing

理论引介 Introduction

当我们第一次去接触一个新的文化，比如美国的一个城市、非洲的一个部落的文化时，如果能够事先了解一些相关的信息，某种程度上可以帮助我们更好地去了解和适应相关文化。这些"相关的信息"常常以旅游小册、校园简介、公众号、媒体短片或新闻报道等形式出现。这些信息对一些我们比较陌生的人群、地方、风俗等做一些归纳性、概括性的总结(generalization)，让我们可以有便捷的、一目了然的把握。我们来看看这些句子：

- 斯里兰卡地处赤道地区，人们的衣着以简单凉快为主。
- 美国人家庭条件还是不错的。
- 厦门鼓浪屿上的院落充满文艺气息。
- 新疆人能歌善舞，热情好客。
- 丹麦人生活在童话般的世界里。
- 由于地处广袤的草原，这里的人民性格热情奔放，生活自然简朴。

这些句子概括性地介绍了一些风俗地貌和人群气质，为人们提供了某种指南。适当的概括性知识是人们尝试去进行跨文化交流的初始阶段。(Baker, 2012: 66) Bennett 认为，尽管出现普遍性被当做刻板印象来应用的问题，在跨文化交流上仍然有必要进行普遍化，否则就会陷入幼稚的个人主义，认为每个人都以完全与众不同的独特方式行动。(贝内特，2012: 41-42)

必要和合适的归纳和概括，无疑对我们认知某一个阶段出现的事物的特征及推测其发展趋势有重要的作用。在跨文化交流过程中，合适的概括性知识可以继续引导人们去尝试倾听，探索未知的文化知识，从而去尊重和共情，愿意进入新的文化环境里去想象和体会，逐渐地，我们就能越来越精细地把握一个文化环境里还存在其它文化多样性。

但人们往往下意识或不自觉地被这些"普遍知识"所引导，变得深信不疑，把概括性

的信息放大到某种标准,成为概念性的认识固化在脑海中,并下意识地用其指导自己的各种决策,他们加上了"所有"、"凡是"、"一定"、"应该都"的概念,开始认为所有的斯里兰卡人都常年穿着简单凉快的衣服,新疆人怎么都能唱两首歌跳几支舞,所有的日本女人应该都温婉含蓄……

这个时候,我们就跌入了"过度概括"(over-generalization)的危谷。因为很明显,这样的认知太绝对、太刻板了。更为重要的是,虽然大家都懂得"不要绝对化"这个道理,但当我们真的遇到一个日本女人时,我们又不自觉地在想,她看上去好"温婉含蓄"啊,到了新疆"一定要和卖葡萄干的大叔跳跳舞",会跟闺蜜说"把娃送到美国交流还是让人放心的,家庭住宿条件不错的","别跟她多啰唆,她是上海人呢"……

所以,"过度概括"这个危谷,不仅仅是在人们偏激绝对的认识中,更是在人们不自觉的日常态度和行为中。其危害来源是由于一个人预先有了定势思维或固化刻板的认知,但和某个真实具体的文化情境出现差异,他因此会惊愕、不解、懊恼、无助。轻则产生误解,重则引发偏见和歧视,带来冲突,原来自己一不小心就成了"杠精"。"没想到这次美国住家条件完全不如我们家!""真后悔娶了个这么彪悍的日本女人,现在我是家里那个百依百顺的好不好!""没想到这个上海女孩现在成了我这个外地打工妹的闺蜜!""我在菲律宾和泰国,并没有看到太多的水果品种,而且价钱跟国内差不多哦~"

When we come into contact with a new culture about, say, an American city, or a region in Africa, it helps us learn about and adapt to the culture if we are acquainted with some relevant knowledge about that culture. Such knowledge may come for example, from brochures, campus flyers, twitters, short films, or news report. We can have a grasp of the local culture with the help of proper generalization of the local people, the places and the customs. Let's take a look at the following sentences:

- Sri Lanka is located near the equator. People wear clothing that is cool and simple.
- American families are relatively well-off.
- Courtyards with artistic flavor are commonly seen on Gulangyu Island in Xiamen.
- People from Xinjiang are renowned for their singing, dancing and hospitality.
- Danish people live in a fairy-tale world.
- Chinese students seldom raise their hands or participate in class discussions when they study abroad.
- People who live on this vast plain are ebullient and lead a simple life.

These sentences provide a general introduction to

第三节　利用概括性知识，同时打破固化刻板的思维
Theme 3　Generalization and non-essentialist perspectives

the local customs and spirit and thus may serve as some kind of guide. Proper generalization is the initial phase that helps people branch out into intercultural communication. (Baker, 2012: 66). Milton J. Bennett believes that "despite the problems with stereotypical use of generalizations, it is necessary in intercultural communication to make the generalizations", otherwise "we may fall prey to naïve individualism, where we assume that every person is acting in some completely unique way." (2013: 58)

Necessary and proper conclusion and generalization will help people to understand better "a thing" that exists for a certain period of time and its developing tendency. In intercultural communication, knowing the basic and rough shape of a culture may lead people to try to listen more carefully, to explore more deeply and to experience more respect and empathy with the diversities in this culture.

However, people tend to be so firmly convinced of such "general knowledge" that they broaden it to the extent that it takes roots in their mind as exclusive concepts and is applied as guidance to decision making, especially when people add words like "all", "every", "should be" or "absolutely". For example, they begin to believe that all Sri Lanka people wear simple and cool clothing all year round; everyone from Xinjiang should be a good singer and graceful dancer; Japanese women are absolutely mild and restrained or discreet.

At this point, we have fallen into the danger of over-generalization. Obviously, the above thinking is too exclusive and stiff. And more importantly, such over-generalized statements are so deeply-rooted that sometimes we are affected even without being conscious. For example, we all know that it would be stupid to think in absolute, but when we really meet a Japanese woman, we just can't stop thinking "she is so gentle". There are numerous similar thoughts in our mind: When you go to Xinjiang you naturally tend to assume that the man who sells raisins should dance very well too; It's a good idea to send children to America as exchange students with home stay conditions because Americans have cozy houses; Don't talk with her anymore, she is from Shanghai...

Presumptions and prejudice come from over-generalization. People may be so preoccupied by the "understanding" of a certain culture that they may lose all the chances to reflect and rethink the situation. Therefore, the danger of over-generalization not only leads to extreme thinking but also affects daily behaviors. It is dangerous because one tends to feel surprised, puzzled, worried or helpless if he/she finds sometimes the reality at variance with his/her deeply rooted orthodoxy or stereotype. It is natural that he/she then will feel puzzled, frustrated, irritated, or will even get involved in a conflict. "Little did I think that some host families in America like the one my daughter stayed with have worse living conditions than we do." "I feel regretful that I had married such a strong-minded, tough and careless Japanese woman. Actually I am the obedient one at home for all these years!" "I didn't realize that this fashionable Shanghai girl would become a close friend of mine. After all, I am just a bread-winner who strives for living in this strange big city!" "Actually I haven't seen many kinds of fruits in the Philippines and Thailand as they said. The prices are more or less the same as in China. The quality looks better in China!"

思考 & 讨论 Reflection and discussion

1. 来说说你有哪些被不经意间过度概括的思维(或者大家平时说的"固定思维")"带到沟里去"的体验吧!

2. 当我们说"非洲人民依然生活在水深火热中"这句话的时候,我们是一种什么态度? 我们忽略了什么?

3. 通过概括性描述来定义事物本质和特征的做法,是科学的还是不科学的? 为什么?

1. Do you want to share your experience of being misled by over-generalization?

2. If we say "the African people are still living in abyss of suffering", do we ignore anything?

3. Is it scientific to define the nature and feature of something by generalized description? Why or why not?

学习者自己的提问和反思 Your own questions and reflections

1. _____
   _____
2. _____
   _____
3. _____
   _____

互动小锦囊 Toolkits for interaction

本质主义追究一个东西从何而来,如何成为这个东西而不是别的东西,也就是寻求这个东西的"本质"。中国学者周宪(2016)在谈论如何界定当代艺术作品的时候,提倡从中国哲学思想里寻找理路,来走出因为本质主义的追问而导致的"何为艺术"的冲突和窘境。他强调,中国哲学打破了非此即彼的二元对立思维模式,转而突出和强调事物之间的相关性。相对于强调事物之间具有对立、矛盾、冲突、排斥的关系,中国哲学认为事物之间存在的是以下三种关系:

1. 相互依存的关系
2. 相互包含的关系

第三节 利用概括性知识,同时打破固化刻板的思维
Theme 3 Generalization and non-essentialist perspectives

3. 相互转换的关系

Essentialism pursues the "essence" or "nature" of an object. It tries to find out what makes an object this particular object and how to distinguish it from other objects. However, Chinese scholar Zhou Xian (2016) borrows Chinese philosophy to discuss the boundary of an art piece and points at the new way out of the dilemma arising from the essentialist exploration of the nature of art. He emphasizes that different from the binary thinking when defining an object, which juxtaposes two components in a dual structure more as contradictory and opposite, Chinese philosophy reveals the relationship of objects as follows:

1. interdependent
2. interrelated
3. interchangeable

中国哲学对事物之间关系的表述
An illustration of the relationship of objects in Chinese philosophy

 互动&体验 Interaction

1. 我们有时在一些跨文化教材里能看到下列文字,你同意吗?哪些内容是过度的概括?

平等是大家公认和追求的目标。美国人非常重视平等,甚至把这一问题上升到了宗教的高度。他们认为,人生来平等,因此所有人都有平等的机会获得成功。即便如此,世界上仍有近90%的人对平等这一概念十分陌生,即便是那些身处底层的人也不认为权势和地位是可以靠奋斗可以得到的。美国人对待本国人与外来者并无二致,因此,初来乍到者可能会略感不适,觉得餐厅服务员,商店或酒店的职员,出租车驾驶员和其他服务的从业者看不起他们,对他们并没有表现出特别的热情,但这些人并无恶意,只是把他们当作"自家人"对待罢了。(Kohls:2009, p.35.)

2. 我们在下面画横线的地方填上一些话,看看被别人"过度概括"所引起的"奇妙"感觉(第一个例子已经给出):

≠我的同事来自长春。她一定喜欢吃玉米。

≠你怎么不把_____放在微波炉里热?前面来的中国人都吃热的,喝热的。(懵神)

≠你从_____来的?我们忘了给你准备素食了。

≠你从_____来的？公司年庆给你安排了一个节目。

≠你去_____吧，谁让你是_____！

≠你还是_____吧，我觉得_____来的人都应该会_____呀。

3. 中国的一些城市如北京、上海、杭州等，已经越来越国际化，文化现象也是越来越缤纷多彩。近年来，上海坊间出现各种"鄙视链""歧视链"的说法，比如，

下午茶歧视链：巴黎水/依云＞手冲咖啡＞现磨咖啡＞星巴克＞外卖奶茶＞保温杯泡枸杞

育儿歧视链：双语学校的＞名校的学霸＞名校的学渣＞普通学校的＞菜场附近学校的＞学而思的

办公室语种歧视链：法语＞英语＞港台腔＞各地方言＞本地话

相亲歧视链：海归房车＞本地有房伪中产＞本地小房私家车贷＞颜值掉地

这些歧视链，是不自觉地建立在"凡是""只要"的逻辑上的：只要你喝手冲咖啡，你就不如喝依云水的；只要你是来自普通学校的孩子，你就不如来自双语学校的。具有这种思维的人心理上可能会有优越感，从而在行为上表现为疏远、轻蔑地谈论等。

但亮点在下面的评论里：

——是否有歧视不知道，只知道纯种上海人是越来越少，外地人是越来越多了，所谓那种大上海自身优越感正逐渐消失，而外来的上海人的确优越感十足。

——讲上海话的人处于鄙视链最底层，真的是这样！

——上海人傻钱多速来！

——答对了，上海话已经沦为底层，我平时像交投暗号一样悄悄说……

——纯熟娱乐～

——一方水土养一方人。提出异议的人本来不身处其中，道不同不相为谋。

——在我们公司法国人说法语那绝对是被鄙视的，汉语都不会说，来中国工作是捣糨糊的吗？

——作为文化大国，我们应该开心滴接受这种歧视链，而不是回避并攻击。

——深深感悟到了每个点。

——不能再赞了：有人的地方就有江湖，江湖的意义就在于歧视链。

哪些评论论证了原来歧视的观点，哪些评论反驳了原来歧视的观点？我们可以细

第三节 利用概括性知识，同时打破固化刻板的思维
Theme 3 Generalization and non-essentialist perspectives

细分析人们不同的评论，每一条体现出了说话人的哪些文化态度？你对这些"歧视链"有什么评论？

1. We may see similar descriptions as follows in some cultural textbooks. Do you agree with them? Do you think some of the statements are over-generalized?

Equality is an announced goal. It is so cherished in the U.S. that it is seen as having a religious basis. Americans believe that all people are created equal and that all should have an equal opportunity to succeed. This concept of equality is strange to seven-eighths of the world, which views status and authority as desirable, even if they happen to be near the bottom of the social order. Since Americans like to treat foreigners "just like anybody else", newcomers to the U.S. should realize that no insult or personal indignity is intended if they are treated in a less than deferential matter by waiters in restaurants, clerks in stores and hotels, taxi drivers, and other service personnel. (Kohls, 2009: 35)

2. Let's fill in the missing words in the following sentences and try to sense how "over-generalization" affects our thinking. (First example is given.)

≠ My <u>colleague</u> is from <u>Changchun</u>. She must <u>like to eat corns</u>.

≠ Why don't you warm _____ in the microwave oven? You people from China always have hot food and drinks.

≠ You come from _____? Sorry, I forgot to prepare vegetarian meal for you.

≠ You are from _____? We have arranged you to sing a song in the company's annual dinner party.

≠ You might as well _____, I think that all people who come from _____ can _____.

3. Some Chinese cities such as Beijing, Shanghai, Hangzhou and so on have become more and more international. A variety of cultural phenomena are seen in these cities. Recently, several "chains of discrimination" (the previous choice is "better" than the next choice) are read in WeChat posts which prevail in Shanghai, such as,

<u>Chain of discrimination on afternoon tea:</u> Paris water/Evian＞freshly ground coffee＞instant coffee＞Starbucks coffee＞take-away milk-tea＞wolf-berry tea in a thermos flask

<u>Chain of discrimination on sending children to schools:</u> study in a bilingual school＞be a top student in a famous school＞be an underachiever in a famous school＞ study in an average school ＞ study in a poorly performing public

school＞study in training institutions like Xueersi

Chain of discrimination on the language spoken in the office: French＞English＞Mandarin with Hong Kong or Taiwan accent＞Shanghai dialect

Chain of discrimination on dating conditions: People returned to home-country after studying abroad who own property and private cars＞middle-class-to-be who own property＞locals who own a small apartment and has bought a car on installments＞plain-looking people

These "chains of discrimination" are some unconscious assumptions based upon simplistic logic of "as long as": You are inferior to the people who drink Evian as long as you have a cup of instant coffee in your hand. As long as you are a student from ordinary schools, you are inferior to those from bi-lingual schools. This kind of feeling superior to others leads to avoidance of communication, prejudice, and discrimination.

But let's read more interesting comments from the readers:

> —I don't know for certain whether the chain of discrimination really exists. What I do know is that the number of locals is comparatively small in contrast with the growing number of outlanders. The locals no longer feel as superior as the new-comers.
>
> —People who speak the local Shanghai dialect are at the bottom of the chain. It's true.
>
> —Shanghainese are rich and stupid. Come here! Hurry!
>
> —This is just for fun.
>
> —The unique features of a local environment always give special characteristics to its inhabitants. People cannot understand the chain of discrimination because they don't live here. Birds of different feathers do not flock together.
>
> —French-speaking people are absolutely discriminated against in our company. If they cannot speak Chinese, why come to China?
>
> —China is a country with many different cultures. We should be able to make peace with the chain instead of attacking or avoiding it.
>
> —I feel exactly the same way as said in those chains.
>
> —I can't agree more: Where there are people, there are chains of discrimination.

Which of the comments prove the existence of the chain of discrimination? Which refute the chain? What do these different comments tell us? What are your coments after reading them?

第三节 利用概括性知识,同时打破固化刻板的思维
Theme 3　Generalization and non-essentialist perspectives

3.2　非文化本质主义的观念和行为
Understanding non-essentialist perspectives

理论引介 Introduction

"本质主义"(essentialism)是一个古老而又深刻的哲学概念,从思想渊源上看,最早可以追溯到柏拉图之前的巴门尼德,他认为世界具有存在和非存在的二元对立关系。(汪子嵩,1997:678 – 679)这一最初的理解后来在中外学者中不断得以深入探讨、维护和反拨。在语言文学和文化领域,"本质主义"也是一个重要和长久研究的话题。在跨文化能力培养与研究中,这一概念在近几十年来受到了质疑和挑战,比如一些社会学家和后殖民主义批评家包括 Hall, Gilroy, Bhabha, Soya 等人就用"混杂"(hybridity)的概念来挑战文化认同的同质化和本质化。(德里克,2011:147 – 154)

学者 Holliday 多年来从语言学、社会学和地缘政治学角度解构了本质主义在文化中的偏激运用,强调非文化本质主义(non-essentialism)观念和行为方式,他和 Kullman 以及 Hyde(2017)共同著书,指出文化本质主义观点依二元对立之名,简化甚至抹杀了具体的、多元的、复杂的、即时的文化差异,因为这种哲学观"假定在某种特定文化中有一个普遍存在的本质、同质性和一致性"(4),而这会导致全球化过程中,对不同文化的群体和个人的判断变得简单粗暴和僵化,制造不真实的文化差异,最终优化自我,盲目树敌,人为构建交流屏障。

欧洲一些学者也比较赞同他的这一基本观点,强调以非文化本质主义为理论框架来进行语言和跨文化教学。如 Hoffman 和 Verdooren(2018:26)就指出,"将文化认定为某种具有清晰界限的、实实在在的'东西',来绝对地割裂不同群体,并决定群体内人们的行为的做法是一种谬误"。

在跨文化交流过程中,出于本质主义的思维模式和行为方式,人们就可能会"在和一个外国人或一个和我们不同的人进行交流时,一定要先了解他们文化中的细节或固

3.2 非文化本质主义的观念和行为
Understanding non-essentialist perspectives

定的评价。"(Holliday, Kullman & Hyde, 2017: 4)虽然 Holliday 等学者对文化本质主义批判的根源和目的要大大超出跨文化交流所探讨的范畴,但他们对文化本质主义的批判,在某种意义上就是对过度概括这种思维方式的批判,好像了解了文化中的细节和固定的评价,就一定能够帮助人们顺利地交流,而没有意识到,一个文化具有异质性,人们的文化身份因不同情境而有所转换,预知的信息有时反而会阻碍了通畅的交流。更为危险的是,本质主义观在强调文化内部的趋同和稳定过程中,突出了与其它文化的差异,往往不自觉地贬低其它文化,引发歧视和偏见。

综合其他学者的观点,我们认为,人们的文化认同其实同时具有两个维度:一个是内部相似趋同的维度,一个是与外部相异糅合的维度,这两个维度是缺一不可的,但在很多时候不容易平衡好,因为人们往往为了保持文化团体内的共性和相似性,保持自身文化的传承性,而去强调与其它文化团体的相异之处,这就很容易导致与其它文化的割裂,甚至会导致优越自身文化,置其它文化于低劣之处,遮目于其它文化的真实内涵;但是,如果太过于趋向认同于其它文化,往往又丢失了自身文化的独特性和稳定性。

因此,在跨文化交流过程中,我们要了解本质主义思维的特点,看清它在某些时候可能导致的危害,尤其是个体与个体交流的时候,并在一定程度上理解和训练非文化本质主义观念和行为方式,以此来纠正文化本质主义带来的交流认知和行为上的偏差。但同时也有学者,如 Arif Dirlik,曾提醒我们更深入地思考本质主义思维:"似乎任何身份接纳,包括可能对任何集体政治行动的形式来说必不可少的身份,都被指控为是本质主义(原文为'都受本质主义的指控'——编者按),所以,常常不清楚到底是反对本质主义本身还是反对政治,在这种情况下,充当诋毁政治的稻草人目标的正是本质主义。"(2011:147-154)

Essentialism is an old philosophical concept with profound meanings. It could date back to pre-Socratic Greek Philosopher, Parmenides of Elea. Parmenides believes that the world is in duality with the existent and non-existent. (Wang, 1997: 678 – 679) This way of understanding the world/things has been probed into, nourished or challenged among domestic and overseas scholars. In domains of philosophy and literature, essentialism has been an important research topic for a long time. However, some researchers of intercultural competence have been doubting and challenging the concept in the past decades, for example, some sociologists and post-colonialists such as Stuart Hall, Paul Gilroy, Homi Bhabha, Edward Soya, analyze in detail the concept of hybridity thus challenge the cultural homogeneity and essentialism. (Dlrllk: 1999:108)

Adrian Holliday for many years has deconstructed essentialism in culture from the aspects of linguistics, sociology and geopolitics, and strongly advocates a non-essentialist way of understanding culture and behaving in intercultural communication. Holliday, Kullman and Hyde (2017: 4) point out that the cultural essentialists have simplified or even negated the

第三节 利用概括性知识,同时打破固化刻板的思维
Theme 3　Generalization and non-essentialist perspectives

specific, diverse, intricate and instant characteristics of intercultural differences in the name of duality. They "presume that there is a universal essence, homogeneity and unity in a particular culture." Such a presumption leads to a simplified and inflexible understanding of cultural groups and individuals, or even "creates" false cultural difference. In doing so, obstacles are built between the two sides of intercultural communication.

Some other European scholars are also supporting the point of views in Holliday's non-essentialist theory and using it as the basic framework in language teaching and intercultural teaching methodologies as well as new research paradigms. As Edwin Hoffman and Arjan Verdooren (2018:26) put it: "thinking that cultures are actual 'things' with clear borders that exclusively separate groups of people and determine their behaviour" is a "fallacy".

Based upon essentialism, "to communicate with someone who is foreign or different we must first understand the details or stereotype of their culture." (Holliday, Kullman & Hyde, 2017: 4) Although the root and purpose of the theory of cultural essentialism is much beyond the scope of intercultural communication, cultural essentialism is to some extent a kind of over-generalization, which assumes that it is a must to know the details and stereotypes of a culture for successful communication. Essentialists don't realize the cultural heterogeneity. They don't realize that cultural heterogeneity dictates that people have different identities in different cultural situations, in which predicted information in fact hinders the communication. To make matters worse, essentialists emphasize internal convergence and stability of a culture and thus highlights its difference with other cultures. In doing so, they tend to belittle other cultures unconsciously, which may result in prejudice and discrimination.

To summarize all the theories, we realize that actually in cultural identification there are two dimensions existing at the same time: one is approaching inwardly to similarities with other members within a cultural group; the other is approaching outwardly to interact with the differences of other people outside the cultural group. Neither of these two dimensions can be neglected. However, on many occasions these two dimensions cannot be balanced well, because when maintaining and inheriting the common values in a cultural group to identify themselves, people at the same time distinguish themselves from other cultures, which might dangerously lead to degrading other cultures and putting their own culture in a superior or even central position, blocking the equal values of other cultures; however, being too open and too interacting with other cultures people might easily lose their own identities. Therefore, in intercultural communication, we need to see clearly the harms cultural essentialism can bring to intercultural communication. We need to learn and practice non-essentialist perspectives to correct the offset of essentialist perspectives in developing intercultural competence. On the other hand, some scholars also remind us to probe more deeply the essentialist way of thinking. For example, Arif Dirlik points out that "(i)t seems like any admission of identity, including the identity that may be necessary to any articulate form of collective political action, is open to charges of essentialism; so that it is often unclear whether the objection is to essentialism *per se*, or to the politics, in which case essentialism serves as a straw target to discredit the politics." (1999:114)

思考 & 讨论 Reflection and discussion

1. 非文化本质主义所反对、强调和提倡的是什么？
2. 是不是强调了非文化本质主义，我们就不可以对一个文化或文化形态给出定义和概括性评价了？

1. What is opposed to, emphasized and encouraged by non-essentialism?
2. Do you agree that we shouldn't define or generalize a culture if we agree with non-essentialism?

学习者自己的提问和反思 Your own questions and reflections

1. _____
   _____
2. _____
   _____
3. _____
   _____

互动小锦囊 Toolkits for interaction

Holliday，Kullman 和 Hyde 合作的 *Intercultural communication: An advanced resource book for students* 一书，对比了文化本质主义和非文化本质主义对文化的不同解读(2017:4)。

第三节 利用概括性知识，同时打破固化刻板的思维
Theme 3 Generalization and non-essentialist perspectives

	本质主义的文化观点	本质主义谈论文化的方式	非本质主义的文化观点	非本质主义谈论文化的方式
（文化的）性质	文化是一种实体，好像是某个人们能够参观的地点。文化具备同质性，某种特征在该团体中普遍分布，人们因此会认为一个团体或社会是简单清晰的。	"假期里我参观了三种文化：西班牙、摩洛哥和突尼斯。"	文化是一股社会力量，哪里呈现得多，哪里就看到的多。社会是一个复杂体，很难准确地归纳其特征。	"我去过的每一个国家在文化上都有差别。"

Holliday, Kullman and Hyde (2017: 4) compare essentialist and non-essentialist perspectives of seeing and talking about culture in their book *Intercultural communication: An advanced resource book for students*.

	Essentialist view of culture	How people talk about it	Non-essentialist view of culture	How people talk about it
Nature (of culture)	"A culture" has a physical entity, as though it is a place, which people can visit. It is homogeneous in that perceived traits are spread evenly, giving the sense of a simple society.	"I visited three cultures while on holidays. They were Spain, Morocco and Tunisia."	Culture is a social force which is evident where it is significant. Society is complex, with characteristics which are difficult to pin down.	"There was something culturally different about each of the countries I visited."

互动＆体验 Interaction

1. 给下面的句子补充新的想法，避免过度概括、过分依赖事物普遍性、简化或消解文化多元性和丰富性的思维模式。可以参照例句，还可以再多举几个例子。

1	朋友约我去印度，那里是不是很脏，到处都是污水，小偷也多啊……	⇒	有些地方的确很脏，但应该有很复杂的历史原因，有些地方也会特别干净。
2	你们法国人不是挺浪漫的吗？	⇒	哦，好吧，法国人跟浪漫好像也没有必然的联系。
3	你肯尼亚来的？来段非洲舞蹈呗～	⇒	
4	你重庆妹子居然不吃辣?！	⇒	
5	你这叫饺子皮？怎么是梯形的?！	⇒	长在中国真不知道，饺子皮还有这么多种形状，真是开眼啊。

续　表

6	中国人嘛,还是脱不了儒家文化啦。	⇒	
7		⇒	
8		⇒	
9		⇒	
10		⇒	

2. 一个文化有时和一个国家、一个民族的概念范畴基本一致,但有时并不一定完全等同。用本质主义的思维方式去描述一个文化,甚至过于宣扬一个国家或民族文化的优秀,其中就会暗含"你我有别""我强你弱",从而下意识地贬低了别的文化。

我们有时会在向外国朋友介绍中国文化的资料或书籍里看到这些说法,我们看看其中隐含的本质主义思维可能带来的文化中心主义。

○ 中华文化是世界上最灿烂优秀的文化。

○ 中国文化历史悠久,上下五千年,内涵极其丰富。

○ 道家的"无为"思想在人类历史上是绝无仅有的,多么高妙啊。

○ 我们可以骄傲地说,老祖宗的文化是最好的!五千年屹立不倒,一定有着深刻的原因。

○ 整个现代西方在音乐、戏剧、建筑、绘画各方面的极简主义,与东方美学关系极深,特别是汉字书法美学。

3. 非文化本质主义认为,在某个具体情境下,人们会产生特定的文化观念和行为,并不受概括性描述的规定,而是呈现出"我中有你""你中有我"的状态,通过这种"穿针引线"的方式,我们可以走出本质主义二元对立引发的人为割裂和刻板规定。试着在四栏里各挑选一个短语,串成一个有逻辑意义的句子。看看你能组成多少这样的句子。

马来西亚的	一个小说家	热情地	对孩子吼叫。
埃及的	一个拳击运动员	焦虑地	开车。
尼日利亚的	一个"家庭妇男"	礼貌地	在医院看病。
中国的	一个老师	一丝不苟地	上下班。
沙特阿拉伯的	一个清洁工	准时准点地	跟同事打招呼。
日本的	一个渔民	有着	丰富的自然地理知识。
瑞士的	一个政府官员	平等地	对待妻子/丈夫。

第三节 利用概括性知识，同时打破固化刻板的思维
Theme 3 Generalization and non-essentialist perspectives

续表

法国的	一个时装模特	有着	黝黑的皮肤。
阿根廷的	一个园丁	有着	雪白的皮肤。
伊朗的	一位女司机	耐心地	对孩子讲故事。

1. Try to add some new ideas in the right column on the basis of the original ideas in the left column in the following table. Avoid over-generalizing, over-universalizing, or simplifying. You can also give more examples.

1	My friend invited me to go to India. Isn't it a dirty country with sewage flowing everywhere? And the thieves ...	⇒	Some places are dirty, probably for some historical reasons. But some places are extremely clean.
2	Aren't you French people romantic?	⇒	Well... French people aren't necessarily romantic...
3	You're from Kenya? Can you perform an African dance?	⇒	
4	You can't eat spicy food! And you are from Chongqing?!	⇒	
5	You call this dumpling wrapper? How come it's ladder-shaped?	⇒	Even though I live in China, I didn't know that dumpling wrappers could be made into so many shapes. What an eye-opener!
6	Chinese people, we'd better behave within Confucius doctrines.	⇒	
7		⇒	
8		⇒	
9		⇒	
10		⇒	

2. A culture sometimes takes the boundary of a country or a nation but sometimes the two things are not identical. To describe a culture in the essentialist way or to highlight, especially with extreme tones, the good qualities of a certain culture suggests superiority to other cultures. As a matter of fact, we often belittle other cultures even without knowing it.

We sometimes read such statements in books on Chinese culture or we even introduce our culture to foreigners in the following ways. Now it's time for us to think about how essentialism may bring about cultural centralism.

★ Chinese culture is the best culture in the world.

★ With 5,000-year historical standing, Chinese culture is of great, great value.

★ The Taoist "inaction" thought is unparalleled in the world history.

★ Thus, we may safely conclude that Chinese culture is the best among all the

3.2 非文化本质主义的观念和行为
Understanding non-essentialist perspectives

civilizations in the world. There must be a reason why the Chinese culture has lasted for 5,000 years!

★ Modern minimalism in western music, drama, architecture, and painting is hardwired with eastern aesthetics, especially Chinese calligraphy.

3. Non-essentialist view of culture upholds that people's perceptions and behaviors in a culture can't be defined by generalized description. We may find something in common in different cultures, if we rid ourselves of the dualistic thinking pattern. Try to pick four phrases respectively from the four columns and connect them into a logical sentence.

A Malaysian	novelist	warmly	shouts at the children.
An Egyptian	boxer	anxiously	drives a car.
A Nigerian	house husband	politely	goes to hospital.
A Chinese	teacher	carefully	goes to work and comes off work.
A Saudi Arabian	garbage man	punctually	greets the colleagues.
A Japanese	fisherman	has	rich knowledge in nature and geography.
A Swiss	government official	equally	treats his wife/her husband.
A French	model	has	dark skin.
An Argentine	gardener	has	white skin.
An Iran	woman-driver	patiently	tells children stories

第三节 利用概括性知识,同时打破固化刻板的思维
Theme 3 Generalization and non-essentialist perspectives

援引阅读 Quoted readings

"后结构主义与后殖民主义学者在反对本质主义的文化差异时,不是要否定或抹杀差异本身,而是否定以二元对立形式表现的、带有价值判断的差异,如母语者/非母语者、个人主义/集体主义、东方主义/西方主义、自我/他者等。本质主义的二元对立不仅不是对差异的肯定,相反是对差异的简化与去历史化,把差异用话语构建为弱势。(Jones,2013)正如Dirlik(1996)所指出的,本质主义其实是对时间、空间的同质化:在空间上忽视个体社会或社群的文化差异,如东方主义对于东方的再现就是忽略了亚洲各个社会的不同文化特性,削弱了他们自身再现的能力;而在时间上又将其固化为某一文化经典,如将儒学等同于中国文化,否认了文化作为生活的经验屈从于时间的生产与再生产。"(第63页)

——冯海颖,黄大网.《跨文化交际研究:从本质主义到批判现实主义》.《外语界》.2016年第1期,61-69页.

"本质主义的总体性,之所以弥漫着太过浓重的独断论色彩,主要原因之一即在于,本质主义无法假设所谓总体性(尤其是生活世界的总体性)终究只是一种假设,其在终极的或最后的意义上是一种既不可证实亦不可证伪之物,因而任何总体性都只具有有限的反思能力。对于一张桌子,我们当然可以借助某种手段或程序,来确证它在总体上是木头做的还是石头做的。我们还可以以思辨的方式来论证它表征着怎样的时代精神,因而具有多么非凡的总体性。但是生活世界显然与之别如天壤,无限的流变性、多样性和复杂性即决定了其在总体的意义上只能是'非课题性'的,因而任何总体性都是某种视角的产物,即某种单一规定性的延伸与拓展,其作为总体性并不具有对于全部生活的现实规定性。所以,我们毋宁将生活世界的总体性看作某种假设,并借助对于假设性的自觉而使关于生活世界的对话成为可能。"(第9页)

——白利鹏.《生活世界:非本质主义的总体性如何可能》.《社会科学研究》.2008年第6期,6-11页.

"We realize that the essential- non-essentialist distinction, like all other dichotomies, is harsh and ignorant of the fact that in reality views range between the two extremes. Nevertheless, essentialism in the way we see people and culture is the same essentialism which drives sexism and racism. The equivalent condition, culturism, (…) similarly reduces and Others the individual and underlies many of the problems in the world today. By Othering we mean imagining someone as alien and different to 'us' in such a way that 'they' are excluded from 'our' 'normal', 'superior' and 'civilised' group."(p.2)

—Holliday, A., Kullman, J., & Hyde, M. (2017). *Intercultural Communication: An Advanced Resource Book for Students*. Milton Park: Routledge.

3.2 非文化本质主义的观念和行为
Understanding non-essentialist perspectives

"本质主义无疑是当代文化研究中最得意的词之一。似乎任何身份接纳,包括可能对任何集体政治行动的形式来说必不可少的身份,都受本质主义的指控,所以,常常不清楚到底是反对本质主义本身还是反对政治,在这种情况下,充当诋毁政治的稻草人目标的正是本质主义。……在极端主义的逻辑里,只能在自由个人主义层面上才能解决对'本质主义'的怀疑,即使如此,也是因为一般的自由至上主义'本质化'了这个主题。……虽然反本质主义的混杂在极端情况下破坏了'抵抗统治'的可能性,同样重要的是它没有与实际世界达成妥协以便应付现实的挑战。"(第147-154页)

——阿里夫·德里克.《历史回归:关于离散、混杂、地点和历史》.何成洲编.《跨学科视野下的文化身份认同》.北京:北京大学出版社,2011年.

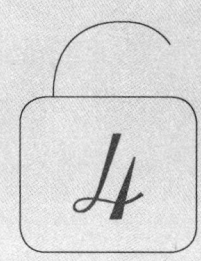

第四节
延迟判断，应对"模糊性"

Theme 4
Delaying judgment and managing ambiguity

第四节 延迟判断,应对"模糊性"
Theme 4　Delaying judgment and managing ambiguity

4.1 延迟你的判断
Delaying your judgment

理论引介 Introduction

当你遇到一个人喋喋不休地抱怨甚至指责时,你的第一反应是什么?立刻反驳?怒怼回去?冷处理?耐心解释?可能都不太能起到有效沟通的作用。当我们逐渐学习到我们可能会被过分概括的知识误导后,我们可以尝试在行动上有所改变。在进入跨文化通道后最初的一个行动,是我们需要"延迟"我们的判断。延迟判断(delaying judgment),也有学者称之为"悬置判断"(suspending judgment),它是一个困难但十分管用的跨文化技巧。

简单来说,延迟判断就是当你在一个多文化环境中感受到和自己不一样的事物或者让自己不舒服的事情时,第一个反应是"停",不要急着下判断、贴标签,比如我们常常听到的"他们就是没文化"、"中国教育就是不如美国教育优秀"、"她就是玩弄你的感情"、"这个意大利公司怎么这么没效率"等。我们不排除判断一件事或一个人的必要

性,但也要意识到,在多文化环境中,有时候我们可能是因为以前的经验、价值观、刻板印象和过度概括而忘记了要根据某个具体情境来判断,变得操之过急,甚至是误判。

如果你愿意考虑延迟你的判断,那我们可以做第二件事,就是把对某件事情的不解和不爽放入"不确定袋子"里,不贴标签。在跨文化交流过程中,"不确定性"是个非常微妙但又绕不过的常见的"坎",不少学者对此都有过专门或简略的研究。不确定性是一种认知过程中的心理现象,适当的不确实性可以引发人们的好奇心和创新精神,但超出人们的承受范围,就不能达到有效交流的目的。(Gudykunst,2014,a:286)在一定的不确定心理状态下,虽然人们心理上有些不舒服,但可以缓解冲突所带来的紧张和焦虑,而且让我们有足够的时间或空间去思考和学习,去搜集更多的信息,学习更多的相关知识,来充分了解让你不爽的各种环境、语言、行为

和态度的深层次原因,增加交流双方的了解和尊重。

"遭遇——放松——延迟判断——放入'不确定袋子'——搜集信息——思考——给出阶段性判断"这样一个新的思维过程和习惯,对很多个性爽快、直接的人,或对某些聪明得"能一眼看透"的人,或对某些事物有坚定信仰的人,尤为是个挑战,但可能却对这些人尤为有用,可以帮助他们从可能的简单粗暴的判断或误判中脱身出来,用平和、开放、客观的新态度看待问题。

When you hear someone babbling on and on about the people they meet on their way of travelling or complaining endlessly about something you have done in a new environment, what is your first reaction? Fight back immediately? Show indifference? Explain patiently? None of these might lead to an effective communication. Now that we comprehend the probability of being misled by some over-generalized knowledge, we need to do something about it. To start with, we may try to delay our judgment in a multicultural environment. Delaying judgment, or "suspending judgment" according to some scholars, is a difficult but helpful skill in improving your intercultural ability.

To put it simply, delaying judgment means we need to pause, and think when we find ourselves in a "different" or even "uncomfortable" situation. Delaying tries to break the habit of making rash judgment or labeling others after we enter an intercultural tunnel. Look out for statements like "They're just undereducated." "Chinese education is no comparison to American education." "This is just the best in the world!" "She is just playing with you in your relationship." "ThisItalian company is so ineffective." There is no denying the fact that judgment is very necessary. However, it is important for us to understand that people easily make unfair or even wrong judgment out of haste, and especially in an intercultural communication process, out of over-generalization, stereotypes, presumptions, and prejudices.

If you are willing to delay your judgment, it's time to go on with the second step, that is, to put all your puzzled and uncomfortable feelings into a "bag of uncertainty". This means you start to "blur" the judgment and get ready psychologically for the possibility that there might be other explanations.

In intercultural communication, the feeling of uncertainty is a subtle, common but normal "threshold". Many scholars have written about it. Certain degree of uncertainty can arouse people's curiosity and creativity but if the feeling of uncertainty is "above our

第四节 延迟判断,应对"模糊性"
Theme 4 Delaying judgment and managing ambiguity

maximum thresholds or below our minimum thresholds, we cannot communicate effectively." (Gudykunst, 2014 a: 286 – 287)

Such a relabeling process does cause some discomfort and tension, but it may reduce the tension and anxiety brought on by intercultural conflict. If we fit the "bag of uncertainty" into our mind, we will win time to listen and study, accumulate more information and form more insights. In that way, we will be able to understand better the intrinsic reasons behind the "uncomfortable" intercultural situations in aspects of language, behavior and attitude. This may be a better way to enhance mutual understanding and respect.

"Encounter-loosen up-delay the judgment-put the issue into a 'bag of uncertainty'-explore and collect more information-reflect-judge for the time being". This thinking pattern may be particularly challenging for people who are straightforward, resolute, "easily see through things" or have good intuition, yet it might be particularly helpful to them also to avoid making hasty and erroneous judgment and to look at problems in a peaceful, open and objective way.

思考 & 讨论 Reflection and discussion

1. 在什么情况下,我们可以鼓励一个"聪明得能一眼看透"的人,或是一个"果断利落"的人,去尝试一下"延迟判断"呢?
2. 在必要时进行"延迟判断",往往带来心理上的不适感。我们如何克服?
3. 什么情况我们必须要做出"一个明确的判断",没有含糊可言?

1. Under what circumstances do we encourage people who "see through things at first sight", "have good insights", or "have resolved mind" to delay their judgment?
2. How to overcome the discomfort brought by "delaying judgment"?
3. In what situation must we "make an explicit judgment" without any ambiguity?

学习者自己的提问和反思 Your own questions and reflections

1. _____

2. _____

3. _____

4.1 延迟你的判断
Delaying your judgment

互动小锦囊 Toolkits for interaction

延迟判断过程中,有一个"不确定袋子"可以帮助我们练习:我们可以按照下面的方式,把不解或冲突放入这个特殊的袋子里:

≥ 我刚才可能有点急着下结论了。
≥ ta 这么做肯定是……吗?
≥ 我最好还是先去问问情况。
≥ 我给自己一天的时间,明天再来决定这个事情。
≥ 他们这么说,不一定是针对我个人。
≥ 我来问问我闺蜜。
≥ 我可能进入"跨文化通道"了,不能用以前的办法解决问题。
≥ 先把这个问题放入"不确定袋子"吧,这件事可能不是马上能解决的,说不定要猴年马月……

对于阶段性得出的结论或判断,我们可以使用下面的开头去给出:

≥就目前来说,我这样认为……
≥这是我现在的判断:
≥从我的角度,我目前认为……
≥就我现在获得的信息,我觉得……
≥据我所知……

In the process of "delaying judgment", we can use the "bag of uncertainty" to help us. Try the following ways of thinking:

≥ I might have been too hasty in making the conclusion.
≥ Is he/she ... in doing so?
≥ I had better ask about it first.
≥ I will give myself a day to think about it. I will make the decision tomorrow.
≥ They say that against me? I'm not sure.
≥ I'm going to ask my best friend about it.
≥ I might have entered the "intercultural tunnel". I shouldn't solve the

"不确定袋子"
A Bag of Uncertainty

第四节 延迟判断，应对"模糊性"
Theme 4　Delaying judgment and managing ambiguity

problem the way I did before.

≥ Let me put the problem in the "bag of uncertainty" first. It is not something that can be solved immediately. God knows how long it will take.

To draw a conclusion or to make a judgment in a certain phase, we may use the following starting sentences:

≥ For the time being, I believe that...
≥ This is my judgment so far:
≥ From my perspective, I think...
≥ From the information I have collected so far I find...
≥ As far as I know...

 互动&体验 Interactions

1. 请你把一件你一直觉得忍无可忍的事情，试着通过互动小锦囊中的一种或几种方式，放入"不确定袋子"中。

2. 在一次公司年会聚餐上，同事们很偶然地交流起了中国各地馄饨皮的形状：
- 正方形
- 长方形
- 圆形
- 菱形
- 梯形
- 三角形

读到那些"奇形怪状"的馄饨皮的时候，你的第一感觉是什么？脸上有什么表情？你小时候吃过或见过的是哪几种形状的馄饨皮？长大后呢？

如果你的反应是荒唐、尖叫、嘲笑、"这个形状怎么包馄饨啊"等，请你用"延迟判断"的方式，保持一种"不解但冷静"的心情，重新读一遍那些形状，然后把它们放入"不确定袋子"中，并试着跟自己说，"我不应该轻易就判断别人而去嘲笑他们，或者反应如此激烈"，"我不确定他们为什么这么做，等我来慢慢弄清楚"。

3. 看见下面这些情景，打抱不平的你过去会怎样反应？如果采用"延迟判断"的方式，你又可能会怎样反应？

← 一个妈妈怎么能对一个又哭又闹的两岁孩子不管不顾，任由他哭了二十分钟,随后还把他的玩具扔出窗外呢?!

⬅ 七十多岁的老母亲拼命敲门,里面的儿子就是拒绝开门。这像话吗?!

⬅ 一位老师用一年级的课本给三年级的学生上课。这老师也太不负责任了!

⬅ 国外有个商店门口竟然写着"禁止中国游客入内",这太侮辱我们中国了!

⬅ 高速公路上大堵车,已经七八个小时了,没有见到一个警察来疏通。很多司机骂起来:"警察效率太低,整个不作为!"

⬅ 闽南文化就是落后,一个妈妈生了孩子,这个孩子就是为家族生的,自己对孩子都没有决定权。这些妈妈要坚持女性主义的独立,跟大家庭抗争!

⬅ 那些参加十三天十国欧洲游的中国人真是不懂旅游。哪有这么玩的!

1. Think about some moments when you have run out of patience, and then try to use the "bag of uncertainty" to reconsider those moments. You may refer to the suggested ways of thinking in the "toolkits for interaction" in 4.1.

2. During a banquet celebrating the New Year, colleagues start talking about the different shapes of wonton skin in China: they may appear in square, rectangle, circle, diamond, ladder shape and even triangle. When you hear of these different shapes of wonton skins, how do you feel? What's your expression like? In which of those shapes did you eat wontons when you were a child? What about when you grow up?

If you think some of the shapes are absurd or even laugh at them, please try to do the following:

→Keep calm even though you don't understand.

→Delay your judgment.

→Put your puzzled feelings about the odd shapes in the "bag of uncertainty".

→Tell yourself, "I shouldn't laugh or make judgment so rashly." "I should take some time to figure it out rather than overreact."

3. How do you react to the following situations in your daily life?

第四节 延迟判断，应对"模糊性"
Theme 4 Delaying judgment and managing ambiguity

⬅ How could that mother let her two-year-old boy crying literally for twenty minutes without doing anything except for throwing his toy out of the window?!

⬅ An old lady who is over seventy is knocking hard on the door. Her son is inside but he refuses to open the door. What can I say?

⬅ A teacher is using a textbook that is supposed to be used for grade three students now in grade one class. What a teacher!

⬅ I saw a sign saying "No Chinese" in front of a shop in a foreign country. Isn't it racism?

⬅ Traffic congestion is really bad on the highway now and it has been so for over seven hours. I haven't seen any traffic policemen around, not even one. The drivers began to complain, "Where are the traffic police? This is nothing but negligence!"

⬅ Some places in Fujian Province in China are so backward. Women do not have the final say over their children. They give birth to their children only for their husband's family. These women must stand up to fight for their independence.

⬅ Those Chinese who take part in the tourist group that travel 10 European countries in 13 days are so crazy! They just don't know what travelling means!

Now try to "delay your judgment" and consider the above situations again.

4.2 应对"模糊性"
Managing ambiguity

理论引介 Introduction

一旦我们把问题放入"不确定袋子"中,我们就人为地、有意识地进入一段感觉"模模糊糊"的状态,这种模糊感会带来心理上的不舒适感。有时,这个过程会长到让你放弃耐心,放弃交流的愿望,甚至放弃学业、工作上的合作或某种亲密关系,觉得这样做不是傻就是脑子有问题,事情不是明摆着嘛!但在跨文化交流过程中,这样一种开放的心态显得尤为重要,需要极大的耐心,这样我们就留出时间和空间去搜集信息,了解更多的背景知识,因为在跨文化这个特定背景中,人们不同的行为背后是不同文化观念,不是那么容易能够很快学习和理解它的来龙去脉,这一切都需要时间。

但有时会出现相反的状况,就是这种模棱两可的状态,不是由于我们主动延迟判断产生的,而是身不由己的,比如在一个新的文化环境里,我们不确定自己的语言和行为是不是得体,会不会得罪人。或者已经意识到两种不同的文化观念仅仅是有差异,而不是孰优孰劣,但反而让自己无从选择和决定,又想照顾对方的感受,又不想让自己难受。

无论在哪种情况下,我们可以勇敢地面对这些"模糊的时刻",不用逃避和惊慌失措,忍受模糊只是暂时的权宜之计,是为了进一步去积极地管理和应对。怎样去管理和应对呢?具体的步骤包括多维度地学习、积极交流、倾听和观察、分析和评估、灵活地想出应对办法等方式。这些在下面的章节中会陆续谈到。

延迟判断,管理模糊状态,把它当作一个挑战,一个更积极建构合作方式或融入环境方式的契机。当你付出努力,完成一次成功的交流后,你会发现,哇,原来这类情况还可以这么处理,大家现在都满意了,好像我也没有太得罪人,原来我可以这么有潜力,这么灵活,这么有勇气!

第四节 延迟判断,应对"模糊性"
Theme 4　Delaying judgment and managing ambiguity

As long as we put our problems in the "uncertain basket", we are likely to fall into an ambiguous state of mind, which may lead to discomfort at heart. Sometimes such ambiguity lasts long enough to make you impatient, or abandon the desire to communicate, or even back out from cooperation or an intimate relationship. You may think "why bother to make such a simple thing so complicated?" or "people who do this must have mental problems!" Nevertheless, in intercultural communication such an open mind can really help us relieve the maladjustment and discomfort. We keep a "bag of uncertainty" because we want to have the time and room to collect and learn more background information. The intricate cultural conceptions behind people's behaviors are difficult to learn about and understand, so it takes tremendous time and effort.

Still we may come across another different situation, that is, we don't fall into the ambiguous state of mind because we deliberately delay the judgment. Rather, sometimes we are forced into it. For example, we are not sure whether our words and behaviors are offensive in a new cultural environment. Or we have realized that there is only difference, not superiority, between two cultures but it's too difficult to find a balance between being understandable to others and upsetting ourselves.

Whichever situation we are in, we should be brave in dealing with such "ambiguous states". Never escape or panic. We need to understand that bearing the ambiguity is only a temporary strategy. We are just trying to find better ways to manage and cope with the situation. But how? The following chapters will help us with specific steps, including multi-perspective exploration, listening and observation, active communication, analysis and assessment, and coming up with flexible solutions.

Regard delaying the judgment and managing the ambiguous state as a challenge, a way to a more constructive and mediated cooperation. Eventually you'll be surprised at how flexible and creative you could be in dealing with various situations. "It seems that now everybody is more satisfied". "It seems that I didn't offend anyone much". "I didn't know I had such potential and I could be so courageous" ... You may say these to yourself in the end.

思考 & 讨论 Reflection and discussion

1. 在跨文化交流中,"模糊性"产生的原因可能有哪些?
2. 根据前面1.1中对文化内涵的讨论,这些"模糊"的事情,会最终清晰起来吗?
3. 积极应对"模糊性"的最终目的是什么?

1. What could be the causes for the feeling of ambiguity in intercultural communication?

2. According to the previous discussion of "culture" in 1.1, do you think the "ambiguous state" will at last become clear?

3. What is the ultimate purpose of actively dealing with "ambiguity"?

学习者自己的提问和反思 Your own questions and reflections

1. _____
2. _____
3. _____

互动小锦囊 Toolkits for interaction

INCA 项目，全称 Intercultural Competence Assessment Project，即跨文化能力测试项目，由 CILT(英国国家语言中心 The National Center for Languages)主持研究，研究专家们来自英国、德国、奥地利和捷克等国，其专业涉及跨文化理论、行为心理学、工程、语言学习、翻译学、管理学等领域。该项目于 2004 年 10 月底完成，主要关注六个方面的跨文化能力：① 行为的灵活性，② 共情能力，③ 宽忍事物模糊性的能力，④ 尊重"他者"，⑤ 交流意识，⑥ 学习其它文化的能力。这个项目受到不少学者的关注。在人们"宽忍事物的模糊性"方面，INCA 项目是这样阐述的：

	基本能力	中级能力	高级能力
宽忍事物的"模糊性"	当模棱两可的感觉发生时，只是单纯地、一次性地应对。他们也许会不知所措，因为这个情况需要相当程度的参与和付出。	已经开始掌握了一套应对模糊性的措施，并且可以少量地参与进去，同时把事物具有模糊性看作是一项挑战。	始终明白事物可能会出现模糊性，并且在它们发生的时候能够宽忍和应对。

The INCA project—Intercultural Competence Assessment Project, is presided by CILT—The National Center for Language, UK, with experts coming from England, Germany, Austria, Czech and other countries, whose research areas cover intercultural theories, behavioral motivation, engineering, language learning, translation studies, administration and so on. The project ended in October, 2004. It mainly concentrated on developing intercultural competence in the following six aspects: ① tolerance of ambiguity, ② behavioral flexibility, ③ communicative awareness, ④ knowledge discovery, ⑤ Respect for otherness, ⑥ Empathy. INCA describes the ability of "tolerance of ambiguity" as follows:

第四节 延迟判断，应对"模糊性"
Theme 4 Delaying judgment and managing ambiguity

	Level 1: Basic	Level 2: Intermediate	Level 3: Full
Tolerance of ambiguity	Deals with ambiguity on a one-off basis, responding to items as they arise. May be overwhelmed by ambiguous situations which imply high involvement.	Has begun to acquire a repertoire of approaches to cope with ambiguities in low-involvement situations. He begins to accept ambiguity as a challenge.	Is constantly aware of the possibility of ambiguity. When it occurs, he/she tolerates and manages it.

INCA Assessor Manual. (2004).

 互动&体验 Interaction

1. "活珠子"到底能不能吃？

你有没有见过或者看别人吃过一些真的非常"奇怪"、"恶心"的食物？很多外地大学生到南京上学后会慢慢见到一种叫"活珠子"的食物。群里讨论中这个话题引起激烈的反响，以下是部分记录：

> A：望了一眼蛋壳里，快要成形的头部和若隐若现的毛发，觉得挺恶心；虽然听同学说味道鲜美，还是不敢尝试。
> B：谈不上不忍心就是觉得有点恐怖，感觉不是很卫生很文明。就像第一次看到带血牛排一样有一点反胃。
> C：感觉看着就很恐怖甚至会恶心，无法理解为什么有人会喜欢吃这种食物，即便听同学说这还是当地特产小吃还是无法接受。
> D：想想，我们吃鸡，也吃鸡蛋，它就是鸡＋鸡蛋，有什么奇怪的
> E：有的时候听别人吐槽南京人吃活珠子，我就在想，如果是觉得吃幼仔很残忍，我们不也吃鱼籽，小鱼干嘛。
> F：看到他吃会觉得很可怕，好像有些还会有毛毛的，没有办法下口。其实我们广东人真的不是什么都吃的。
> G：广东人不是什么都吃＋1
> H：在壳里蜷缩的样子容易让人想象到母亲怀孕的时候肚子里的宝宝的样子。但是表妹说味道很可口鲜美。emm 表妹和我一样都是温州的，不过她很小的时候去了绍兴，绍兴那边也有活珠子。
> I：是小鸡啊
> J：作为一个吃过人胎盘的在广东长大的人，我也接受不了活珠子……之前军训的时候经常遇上孵化半成型的鸡蛋，若吃下去，茹毛饮血……
> A：想想其实也没啥，以后吃吃看

L：Dei.
D：那个应该是长不大的有问题的小鸡……
H：哦,长知识了。

这个讨论中,

→是不是所有的人都对"活珠子"表示反感?
→同样反感和不解的人,他们在态度上有哪些区别?
→哪位同学吃过比"活珠子"更"可怕"的东西?
→除了南京人,还有哪些地方的人也吃"活珠子"?
→哪些同学后来改变了态度?
→你对这件事情的态度是始终坚决的,还是慢慢模糊了?
→"活珠子"到底能不能吃?从"延迟判断"和"应对模糊性"的角度,我们可以怎么做?

2. Sherley是中国四川人,她和一个德国小伙子Andy正在谈恋爱。一天,Andy跟她聊天时无意中说起,在自己的家乡有一种浴室,是裸体公共桑拿。他也去玩过几次。说者无心,听者有意,Sherley立马跳起来:"你真的好下流啊!"随后几天都没有理会Andy。Andy不断跟她解释,Sherley决定把这件事先放入"不确定袋子",然后自己上网去搜一搜。这一搜不要紧,网上铺天盖地世界各种"奔放"、"麻辣"、"酸爽"的洗浴方式,让她惊呼自己"没见过世面"。你可以跟Sherley一起去查一查,下面这些洗浴方式都出现在世界什么地方,你目前能接受哪些。对于你还不能接受的方式,你愿意继续查一查背后的成因吗?还有,你想尝试哪几种新奇的洗浴方式?

√ 在河里和"尸体"一起清洁和升天。
√ 一边泡澡一边用树枝抽打身体。
√ 平时裹得太严,澡堂是婆婆们目测未来儿媳妇的好去处。
√ 男女共浴,脸不红,心不跳。
√ 节假日亲友家庭聚会,必须去澡堂。
√ 从河里挖出黑乎乎的泥巴涂满全身。
√ 浴娘全身抹上肥皂,再用她身上的肥皂帮你搓澡,使你飘飘欲仙。

第四节 延迟判断，应对"模糊性"
Theme 4 Delaying judgment and managing ambiguity

3. Georgia 在美国生活已经三十年了。但时至今日，她每次回国探亲，送礼物都是她的一件心事。在美国，她和亲友之间送礼物一般不会看重礼物的价值，而她觉得国内的朋友还是相当看重礼物本身的价值。她不知道这个分寸怎么把握，送轻了怕满足不了对方心里的"价值期待"，送得贵重又怕他们觉得她在美国生活优越，"炫富"。

你说说，她这种"战战兢兢"的感觉从哪来？

→个人性格比较谨慎，怕得罪人？
→把现在中国人接受礼物的心理"刻板印象化"了？
→中美文化的确有这种差异，让她烦恼？
→很多中国人至今认为美国生活优越于中国，对她送的礼物有想法，是他们自己自卑感的投射？
→是 Georgia 想得太多，是她自身在美国生活优越感在送礼物这件事上的投射？

还可能是什么原因？

那么，Georgia 该怎样来应对送礼物这件事里她感到的"模糊性"？

→不要害怕和烦恼这种模糊的状态，知道它是有原因的，相信自己可以慢慢积累经验，解决好。
→既然是好朋友，就多问问他们收到礼物后的感觉，了解他们的真实想法，也许并不是她想象的那样。
→这种状态很难消除，Georgia 要适应和接受这种不确定性，与之欣然共存。
→有些人的做法的确一时很难改变，Georgia 可以远离他们。
→多了解美国和中国的实际情况，消除自身的优越感，这样话里话外自然会有平实的口吻，不会引起别人反感。
→送礼物时可以说："这个国内没有，不过中国也有好多东西美国没有哦。下次记得送我。"

还有什么？

1. Are "eggs with legs" edible?

Have you seen other people eat some really "strange" or "disgusting" food? Many university students may notice a kind of local food called "eggs with legs" when they first come to study in Nanjing. A heated discussion took place in a QQ group. The following is a record of part of their discussion.

A: I took a glance into the shell and saw the head and feather of the dead chicken. I thought it so disgusting. My classmates told me that they are delicious but I wouldn't try.

B: I just thought it "horrible" but not disgusting. And I have a feeling that such food is not "clean" or civilized to eat. It reminds me of the churning stomach when I saw bloody steak for the first time. 😱

C: It looks horrible even disgusting. I can't understand why people like eating such food. Even though my classmates told me it's a local snack, I still can't understand.

D: Just think: we eat both chicken and eggs. It's just chicken inside eggs. Why do you feel it strange to eat them?

E: I sometimes hear people say it is disgusting to eat "eggs with legs". I can't help but think if they feel it cruel to eat the hatchling, how come they eat fish eggs and minnows?

F: I feel scared when I see them eating "eggs with legs". Some of them are even fluffy. I just cannot eat them. We Cantonese don't eat everything, really.

G: I agree. We Cantonese don't eat everything.

H: The chick crouching in the egg is easily associated with babies in mother's womb. But my cousin told me it's very delicious. My cousin and I are both from Wenzhou. But she has been to Shaoxing, where people also eat "eggs with legs". 😄

I: They're baby chickens.

J: As a Cantonese who grew up in Guangzhou and has eaten human placenta, I cannot eat "eggs with legs". I've seen people eating them. For me, it's like eating the raw meat and drinking the blood. 😨

A: Give it a second think, it's no big deal. I will have a try in the future.

D: They should be troubled embryos. They can never grow up.

H: Oh, I've learned something.

During the discussion:

→Does everyone show an unwelcome attitude towards eating "eggs with legs"?

→Between the people who feel disgusted and those who don't understand, is there any difference in their attitudes?

→Who has eaten anything even more "horrible" than "eggs with legs" according to the speaker?

→Except in Nanjing, where else do people eat "eggs with legs"?

→How many of the students changed their attitude by the end of the conversation?

→ How about your attitude? Do you insist on your opinions or do you

第四节 延迟判断，应对"模糊性"
Theme 4 Delaying judgment and managing ambiguity

become ambiguous?

→Are "eggs with legs" edible at all? If we understand it from the perspective of "delaying judgment" and "managing ambiguity", what can we do?

2. Shirley is from Sichuan, China. She is in a relationship with Andy, a young man from Germany. One day, Andy talked about a public bathing house in his hometown, where both men and women are allowed to bathe in the same place. He himself had been there several times. The speaker had no particular intention in saying so, but the listener read her own meaning into it. Shirley cried out immediately, "I didn't know you were so indecent!" For the following few days she refused to talk to Andy. Andy kept explaining to her and then she decided to put this issue first into the "bag of uncertainty" and she browsed on the Internet. Then she was astounded at the various bathing styles from all over the world, which are uninhibited, stimulating or refreshing. Shirley began to regard herself as ignorant and inexperienced.

We can search the Internet together with Shirley and try to find out where the following bathing styles come from. How many of them can you accept? How many can you not accept? Are you willing to go deeper to find out the causes of your acceptance or refusal? Besides, which of the novel ways would you like to try?

- √ Bathing with corpse in the river to clean yourself and go to heaven.
- √ Bathing while being whipped with branches.
- √ A Bathhouse is an ideal place for the mother-in-law-to-be to pick up her daughter-in-law. You know, women wear too many clothes outside the bathhouse.
- √ Men and women bathe together without a flush on their face or a fast-beating heart.
- √ Going to the bathhouse is a must at family reunion during holidays.
- √ Cover yourselves with the black mud from the river.
- √ Bathing girl covers herself with soap and serves you. You are now floating on air.

3. Georgia is a Chinese American who has been living in America for thirty years. Every time when she comes back to China to visit family and friends, she finds it a burden to send gifts. In America, many people don't care about the price of gifts as much as Chinese people do. She doesn't know how to choose a proper gift. If the gift is too cheap, she is afraid that the receiver may think he/she is not important for her. If it's too expensive, she is afraid that the receiver may think she is showing off.

As far as you are concerned, why is she so "careful and hesitant"?

4.2 应对"模糊性"
Managing ambiguity

→ She is cautious and tries to avoid offending people as much as possible.

→ She is stereotyping Chinese people's attitude towards receiving gifts.

→ She is troubled by the cultural difference between China and America.

→ Many Chinese people still believe that Americans live a better life than Chinese people and this kind of thinking is projected onto their attitudes towards the gifts.

→ Georgia thinks about it too much. Her concern, in fact, reflects her superiority as an American.

What other possible reasons are there?
Then, how can we help Georgia deal with the 'ambiguity' in sending gifts?

→ Don't be afraid or worry about the ambiguous state. We should understand that there must be a reason behind the ambiguity. We are able to solve the problem when we gather enough experience.

→ Since that they are good friends, Georgia can ask them about their feelings. Things may not be what she thought they were.

→ It is difficult to get rid of such an ambiguous state. Georgia has to adjust to and accept the uncertainty and make peace with it.

→ It is difficult to change others. Georgia had better stay away from them.

→ Learn more about America and China and reflect on her superiority. Talk to others in a more sincere way. Then it is unlikely to offend others in the future.

→ When she sends gifts to others, she can tell them, "It is not sold in China. But there are also many things in China that are not sold in America. I am happy to receive them as gifts next time."

What other ways can you think of to help Georgia?

第四节 延迟判断,应对"模糊性"
Theme 4 Delaying judgment and managing ambiguity

援引阅读 Quoted readings

"'难得糊涂'思想并非郑燮所独创,作为一种思想文化,它已经在中国大地上存在了几千年,其思维方式、生存状态与中国文化所标的的思维方式和生存状态是正相一致的。……'难得糊涂'思想所标的的思维方式,正好是中国文化所特有的'实践理性'的思维方式。传统中国文化不是理性的哲学与科学文化,而是表现性(感性)极强的'艺术化'文化。这种文化的特点在于,不对客观事物进行科学的分析研究,而是停留在对客观事物的感性认识上,即对可感知的客观事物的存在规律进行简单的、普通意义上的归纳与总结。中国文化的这种思维特点,李泽厚先生称之为'实践理性'的思维方式。这种'实践理性'的思维方式,既是理性(聪明)的,同时,它又是反理性(糊涂)的;它是一种居于实践经验的总结;而非逻辑性的分析与研究。因此,在中国文化中,在'实践理性'精神指导下,人们对客观事物的认知是'有限'的:当'这种认知'达到一定'高度'(聪明)时,人们不是继续深究下去,以求终极真理(大聪明、更聪明),而是自然而然地进行了某种意义上的回归('糊涂')。"(第72-73页)

——李少龙.《中国传统文化中的"难得糊涂"思想》.《南开学报(哲学社会科学版)》. 2005年第6期,70-79页.

"Since members of foreign cultures show different ways of behaviour, have different standards and have different opinions, a lot of uncertainty and unpredictability emerges for an individual. The person who is acting in such an intercultural situation often does not know which behaviour is expected and how behaviour is evaluated. For instance, the temporal order of action or the division of labour in other cultures differ from those of one's own culture. Tolerance for ambiguity means to be able to accept such uncertainties and ambiguities, and to find solutions to problems which they might create.

In contrast, persons with a low degree of tolerance for ambiguity experience unstructured and ambiguous situations as unpleasant and threatening. They either try to avoid such situations or to get out of them as soon as possible. If this is impossible, they feel visibly uncomfortable, misinterpret unclear situations, and simplify ambiguities. When trying to solve such problems, they often neglect a part of the problem and search for simple solutions. When confronted with contradictory and ambiguous opinions they search for a compromise and prefer a very clear and definite way of proceeding."(p.4)

— INCA, The Theory. (2004). Retrieved from https://ec.europa.eu/migrant-integration/librarydoc/the-inca-project-intercultural-competence-assessment.

"We cannot interact effectively with host nationals or adjust to the host culture if our anxiety and uncertainly are too high or too low. The optimal level of anxiety and uncertainty that facilitates effective interaction and adjustment is somewhere between our minimum and maximum thresholds. For uncertainty, our optimal level is when we think that host nationals' behavior is predictable, but we also recognize that we may not be able to explain their behavior accurately [...] For anxiety, our optimal level is when we feel comfortable interacting with host nationals, but we still have sufficient anxiety that we are not complacent in our interaction with them."(p.443)

——Gudykunst, W. B. (2014, b). An anxiety/uncertainty management (AUM) theory of strangers' intercultural adjustment. In Gudykunst, W. B. (Ed.), *Theorizing About Intercultural Communication* (pp.419 - 457). Shanghai: Shanghai Foreign Language Education Press.

"When discussing the workings and impact of culture, it is essential to point out that there are always factors which are *not* cultural in nature...

Being part of a social class brings with it certain cultural habits, values and heroes, but also socio-economic aspects such as income and access to housing, education and healthcare. Parents who do not allow their child to go on a school trip are not necessarily motivated by ideas about education or upbringing, but perhaps by the fact that they cannot afford to pay for it. A young man who rebels against his teachers is not necessarily motivated by "youth culture" but is also "just" a teenager, with all the biological and psychological changes that this brings about."(p.39)

——Hoffman, E., & Verdooren, A. (2018). *Diversity Competence*. Bussum: Uitgeverij Coutinho.

第五节
多角度了解信息和认知问题

Theme 5
Multi-perspective exploring and understanding

5.1 多角度了解信息
Exploring with multiple perspectives

 理论引介 Introduction

在我们延迟判断之后,我们就可以利用这个当口,去积极地倾听、阅读、对话,了解更多的背景信息,从而获得较为全面的认知,然后再去找出应对办法。不经过这一个多角度学习的阶段而简单处理问题,是有危害的。

带有单一角度的种种思维及其危害情形包括:

- 不了解情况就简单判断
- 根据以往经验下意识地应对
- 从表面现象看问题
- 过早/过激/过急地贴标签
- 完全根据自己的经验和文化价值观念直接判断
- 负面的刻板印象
- 偏见、成见和歧视
- 文化中心主义
- 极权主义
- 种族主义
- 教条主义
- 过分概括和定性

在你有了自己成熟、稳定、"笃定"的文化观念和信仰后,你是否仍然愿意去慢慢意识到一件事——很多事情发生的原因、背景、经过、结果都是历史的、情境的、复杂多变的,尤其是跟文化相关的现象。这儿有个有趣的事情:曾经有一个"白种人"学生和一个"黄种人"学生住一个宿舍。夏天当他们坐在一起时,他们突然发现,"黄种人"学生的皮肤,无论是胳膊还是腿部、腹部,其实都比那个"白种人"学生"白"。

我们发现,由于文化异质性、文化多样性、文化相对性、文化的流动、越界等因素,各种文化现象呈现出立体、动态、丰富、复杂的特性。因此,仅仅用我们自己的标准去判断别人,是不是可能会是简单、武断、主观、僵化的?

尝试多角度了解信息后,我们可能会在坚持自己观念的同时,改变过去面对不同观点时的强硬态度,或者哪怕不改变,也会有所缓和,能够较好地理解和尊重别人的想法、做法,甚至去感受文化多样性和相对性带给我们的惊喜,感受自己眼界和心胸的不断扩展,感受自己思维的不断深刻和文化调适能力的不断增加,不再被不满或无助的情绪困扰,心里也不再有那么多厌恶和无奈。

多角度了解信息,包括:① 对别人不同于我们的思想、语言、态度、行为举止背后文化原因在深度上的了解;② 对某一个文化事件多角度地认识;③ 对同一个文化现象长时间地跟踪观察、学习。而了解信息的角度包括各种媒体、各种文化表现方式(如艺术、文学、制度、礼仪规范等)、面对面交流、各种通讯方式的交流等。

在当今媒体发达的情况下,每个媒体其实都有着自己的"导向性声音"。我们应该意识到以下几点:① 一个媒体往往带着一个角度去阐释社会文化现象,有些媒体报道的角度相同或相似,有些则差别很大;② 只读一篇文章或报道往往是不够的,要听到真正"不同的声音"(而不仅仅是多看几份类似角度的文章和报道);③ 有些信息是虚假的、不全面的、被隐藏的、不清晰的、暂时的,因此要带着质疑的思维,争取"合成"出一个相对清晰、相对真实、相对全面、相对稳定的"真相"。

After we delay the judgment, we need to use this opportunity to actively listen, read and carry out dialogues so that we can get a relatively deep understanding of the cultural background, the values behind, the motivation of the communication of the interlocutors before finding out proper solutions. It is harmful to solve problems in a reduced and simplified way, without going through this multi-perspective exploring process. The following occasions include harmful mono-perspective understanding.

- Making simple judgment without understanding
- Solving problems with former experiences
- Looking at problems only on the surface
- Labeling too early/rashly/hastily
- Judging and labeling purely from one's own experience and cultural values
- Negative stereotyping
- Prejudice and discrimination

第五节 多角度了解信息和认知问题
Theme 5 Multi-perspective exploring and understanding

- Cultural centralism
- Totalitarianism
- Racism
- Dogmatism
- Over-generalization

When you have acquired your own mature, stable and "self-assured" cultural values and beliefs, are you still willing to take your time to closely examine one cultural phenomenon? The cause, background, development and outcome of many things are actually historical, contextual, complex and volatile, which is especially true for cultural phenomena. There is a story about a "white" student and a "yellow-skinned" student. When summer comes, they sit together and find that the skin of the arms, legs and belly of the "yellow-skinned" student actually looks "whiter" than that of the "white" student.

We gradually realize that because of the heterogeneity, diversity, relativity, fluidity, and hybridity of culture, different cultures may display multiple dimensionalities, dynamic states and complex varieties.

Therefore it would seem too simple, arbitrary, subjective and rigid to judge others solely with our own standards.

After trying to get information from multiple perspectives, we may change our past attitudes towards others' different views while maintaining our own views. Even if we won't change our mind, we may ease the tension so that we can better understand and respect others' idea and practice. We may even enjoy the happy surprises brought by cultural diversity and relativity and experience the constant enhancement of our approach to the "truth". In that way, we will, to some extent, ease our feelings of dissatisfaction, helplessness, disgust, or hopelessness.

Getting information from multiple perspectives includes the following:

(1) Contextually understanding others' ideas, languages, attitudes and behaviors that are different from ours;

(2) Studying a cultural phenomenon from multiple angles;

(3) Exploring a cultural phenomenon through long-term tracking and observation.

The ways we get information include mass media, different cultural representations (e.g. art, literature, institution, norms of etiquette), face-to-face communication, and communication through technical devices, etc.

Media hold "guiding voices". Therefore, we should realize that every commentator, correspondent, or columnist, tends to "report" or comment on social and cultural phenomena more or less with some presumptions. Some reports share similar perspectives to our own, while others are hugely different. So it is far from enough to explore something just by reading one article or report. We should listen to "different voices" (which does not mean reading some articles and reports with similar perspectives). Also some information is false, incomplete, hidden or vague so that we have to remain critical and try our best to "piece together" a relatively clear, authentic, and stable "fact".

思考讨论 Reflection and discussion

1. 经验在什么时候对我们是帮助？什么时候又变成了阻碍？
2. 当我们坚持一个文化观念的时候，我们怎样确定什么时候这种坚持是一种坚定的信仰，什么时候是一种偏激和狭隘的固守？
3. 多角度了解信息，会不会更加扰乱我们的视听，让我们无所适从？为什么？

1. When is experience helpful to us? When will it become an obstacle?
2. When someone insists on a cultural value, when can we say he/she is holding on to a belief and when can we say he/she is holding on to a narrow, rigid understanding?
3. Will multi-perspective exploration confuse us more and make us unable to judge and act? Why?

学习者自己的提问和反思 Your own questions and reflections

1. _____
   _____
2. _____
   _____
3. _____
   _____

互动小锦囊 Toolkits for interaction

在多角度了解信息过程中，我们可以依照下面这个流程来做（Yu & Van Maele, 2018: 364）。这个流程表涵盖了整个过程中需要注意的步骤和技巧，包括：① 搜集和选择需要的信息，② 理解分析信息内容，③ 比较不同角度对同一话题的理解阐述，④ 质疑、反思和总结，⑤ 从对比不同角度来体验移情和尊重。

In our attempt to get information from multiple perspectives, we can refer to the following flow chart which includes the noteworthy steps and skills necessary in the process: ① gathering and selecting the information needed, ② comprehending and analyzing the information, ③ comparing the understanding and explanation of the same issue from

第五节 多角度了解信息和认知问题
Theme 5 Multi-perspective exploring and understanding

different perspectives, ④ questioning, reflecting and summarizing, ⑤ experiencing empathy and respect by exploring from different perspectives.

(1) 浏览+ 摘选	(1) scanning & selecting
⬇	⬇
(2) 理解+ 概括	(2) comprehending & summarizing
⬇	⬇
(3) 分析+ 比较	(3) analyzing & comparing
⬇	⬇
(4) 反思+ 评估	(4) reflecting & evaluating
⬇	⬇
(5) 移情+ 尊重	(5) empathizing & respecting

多角度搜集了解信息和认知事物流程图
A flow of multi-perspective exploring and understanding

互动&体验 Interactions

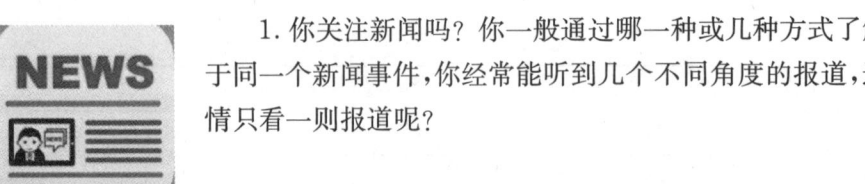

1. 你关注新闻吗？你一般通过哪一种或几种方式了解新闻？关于同一个新闻事件,你经常能听到几个不同角度的报道,还是每件事情只看一则报道呢？

2. 请在你的朋友圈里找一个大家在讨论的话题,比如有关服装或美食的。然后找一找,关于这个话题,在同一个群里都是怎么讨论的。有不同的声音出现吗？有几种不同的声音出现？出现不同声音时大家的反应和表现是怎样的？你觉得通过什么方法可以获得更多相关的观点和信息？

3. 皮草在纽约、巴黎、米兰时装界被广泛运用,但同时也受到一些当地环保主义组织的强烈反对。你本人反对还是不反对使用皮草？请你去从不同角度搜集一些资料,至少从3个角度了解下不同行业的人对皮草使用的看法。这些角度可以包括：

- 时装设计师
- 环保主义者
- 时装裁剪制作者
- 动物学家

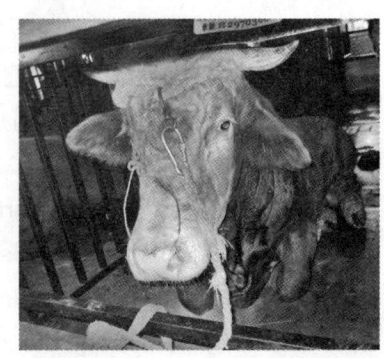

- 有过打猎经验的人
- 环保政策制定者

在了解学习过程中，你是更坚定了原来的想法，还是稍微调整了些原来的想法？你对皮草使用的"真相"是否有了一定的认识？你是否觉得今后如果遇到一个坚定的废除皮草者或坚定的皮草使用者时，你会感觉放松自在些吗？

1. Do you read news? In what way or ways do you read news? On the same news event, do you often read reports from several different newspapers, or read from just one newspaper?

2. Try to check one of your WhatsApp friends groups. Take a look at a recent "hot issue" discussed in this group. Is there any disagreement? How many different voices are there? How do people react and respond to different voices? You can check again whether this issue is also discussed in other groups. What do your friends say in these other groups?

If you find that for one issue, there is only one group or one voice in discussion, how do you think can you get more different opinions and information?

3. Fur is widely used in the fashion world nowadays, but it is also strongly opposed by some local and international environmentalist organizations. Do you object or not object to the use of fur? Please collect some information from different sources to explore the views of people in different professions on the use of fur. These perspectives can include that of:

- a fashion designer
- an environmentalist
- a fashion tailor and producer
- a zoologist
- people with hunting experience
- an environmental policy maker

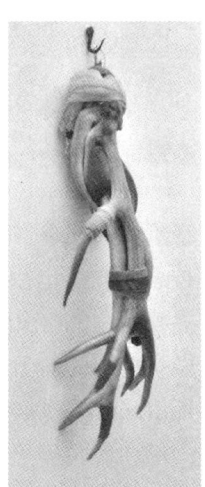

In the process of exploring, did you reinforce your original idea or slightly adjust it? Does your exploration in the "truth" on fur use have a certain conclusion? Do you think you will feel a little more relaxed when you encounter a firm abolitionist of fur or a firm fur user in the future?

第五节 多角度了解信息和认知问题
Theme 5 Multi-perspective exploring and understanding

5.2 多角度认知问题
Understanding with multi-perspectives

理论引介 Introduction

如果能够多角度地了解信息,我们就可以尝试去"多角度地认知问题"了。"多角度认知"当然反对的是单一角度的认知方式,包括5.1部分一开始列举的那些。

人类学家Geertz(1973:3-30)曾借用Ryle"厚实描述"(thick description)这个概念,来讨论如何深度理解和揭示人类某些具体的社会行为特征。Holliday(2013)也借鉴这个概念并将它延伸到跨文化研究领域,将它表述为是"将一个社会现象的不同方面联接起来,从而领悟这个现象更为深刻和复杂的含义"(173)。

当我们认为一件令人惊诧的事情也和其它事情一样是可以理解的,当我们在和不同的人、文化现象或文化事件遭遇时能够学习它们背后的复杂成因,我们就开始了"深度描述"。这种思维方式包括两个方面:① 从一个广阔的视野中拼接不同角度但相互联系的信息来寻找事物的含义;② 在一个社会现象不断演变的过程中去探知它,这些不断演变的现象可能一时看上去彼此没有关联,而且可能让人感到不适和诧异(Holliday,Hyde & Kullman,2004:8)。

在多角度了解信息和深度描述的基础上,我们可以开始一种"多角度认知"。我们认为,多角度认知除了包含在同一个时间或空间里拼接不同角度的信息以及在一段时间或不同空间内跟踪事物的发展演变之外,还可以包含这样一些内涵,比如:

(1)对一个文化概念在一个团体内不断演变的认知的描述;
(2)对一个文化概念在不同团体内不同认知的描述;
(3)对一个文化现象可能存在的相对矛盾的角度的同时描述和认可;
(4)对一个文化现象持久的"模糊性"和"复杂性"的自觉、接纳和探究;

等等。

和其它跨文化技巧一样，"多角度认知"往往是说起来容易做起来难，因为它要"人为地使事情复杂化"。而由于各种原因，我们在日常生活中处理应对文化不适时，往往趋于简单、舒服，会下意识地采取"通常"的做法。因此，要改变这个"通常"的习惯，用复杂的眼光看待事物，需要一个持续的体验过程。

If we can collect information through multiple perspectives, we can try to understand a social or cultural phenomenon with multiple perspectives. "Understanding with multi-perspectives" certainly opposes a simplified and reduced way of thinking, including those listed at the beginning of theme 5.1.

Anthropologist Clifford Geertz (1993) borrows Gilbert Ryle's "thick description" to explain how we should interpret and understand a human behavior in a deeper and more complex way (3–30). Adrian Holliday (2013) draws on the concept of "thick description" in intercultural studies. He briefly describes it as "interconnecting different facets of a social phenomenon to arrive at deeper complexity of meanings" (173).

If we believe that something unexpected could be as comprehensible as the expected things, and if we try to explore the complex causes behind different people's behaviors, we start a "deep description". According to Holliday, Hyde & Kullman (2004: 8) this way of thinking includes two aspects: ① deriving meaning from a broad view of social phenomena, which pieces together different, interconnected perspectives; ② exploration, in which we make sense from an ongoing emergence of social phenomena, which may not immediately seem to connect, and which may indeed be unexpected.

Based on multi-perspective exploring and thick description, we can begin to acquire a "multi-perspective understanding". In addition to the idea of piecing together multi-perspective information in a certain period of time and in the same space, and tracking the evolution in the following time and in different places, this concept can also include connotations as:

(1) an understanding and description of the evolving perception of a cultural phenomemon within a group;

(2) an understanding and description of the different cognitions of a cultural phenomemon within different groups;

(3) an understanding and description of the juxtaposition of the relatively contradictory

perspectives that a cultural phenomenon may possess;

(4) an awareness, acceptance and inquiry of the persistent "vagueness" and "complexity" of a cultural phenomenon.

Like other intercultural skills, "multi-perspective understanding" is often easier said than done because it "artificially complicates things". For various reasons, when we deal with troublesome cultural issues in our daily lives, we often prefer the simple, comfortable ways of explanation and subconsciously adopt the "normal" approach of understanding. Therefore, to change this "normal" habit and view things with a sophisticated eye, we need to practice continuously.

思考 & 讨论 Reflection and discussion

1."对一个文化现象可能存在的相对矛盾的角度的同时描述和认可",是一个伪命题吗？

2. 我们看电影,可能到现在还在用"好人""坏人"来评价一个角色。这样的评价有什么问题？

3."男大当婚,女大当嫁"这个中国传统说法,在现在有着怎样的不同观点？这些观点有无优劣之分？

1. Is it a false proposition that "a description and recognition of the relatively contradictory perspectives of a cultural phenomenon may exist simutaneously"?

2. When we watch movies, some people may still use "a good guy" and "a bad guy" to evaluate a character. What is the problem with this?

3. A traditional Chinese saying goes that, "Upon growing up, every male should take a wife and every female should take a husband". What different views about marriage are there today in your country? Are some of those views "better" than others?

学习者自己的提问和反思 Your own questions and reflections

1. _____

2. _____

3. _____

5.2 多角度认知问题
Understanding with multi-perspectives

互动小锦囊 Toolkits for interaction

Holliday，Hyde & Kullman（2004：8）用下面这个图表来勾勒跨文化领域的"深度描述"概念。这个图表简洁地表述了一个人的自我认知与社会的复杂性、文化的多样性之间的相互关系，并说明，由于这些互动关系的存在，我们必须"深度描述"一些人们身上出乎我们意料的表现。

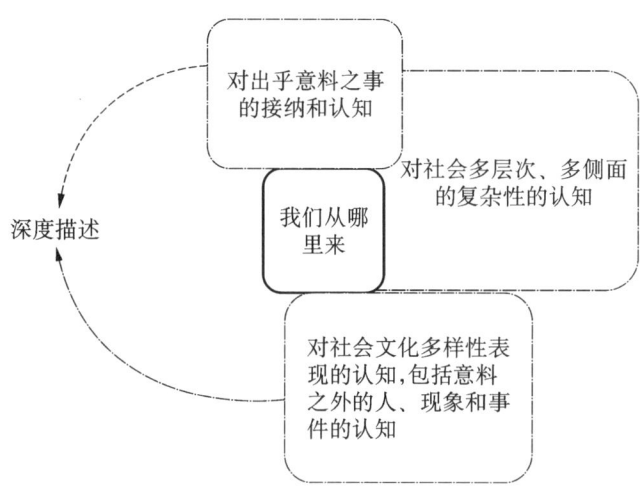

Holiday, Hyde and Kullman (2004: 8) use the following figure to illustrate "thick description" in intercultural competence development. It briefly reveals the interactive relationship between the society, representations of the society, behaviors of an individual and his/her own identity. It explains why "thick description" is needed when we see something "unexpected".

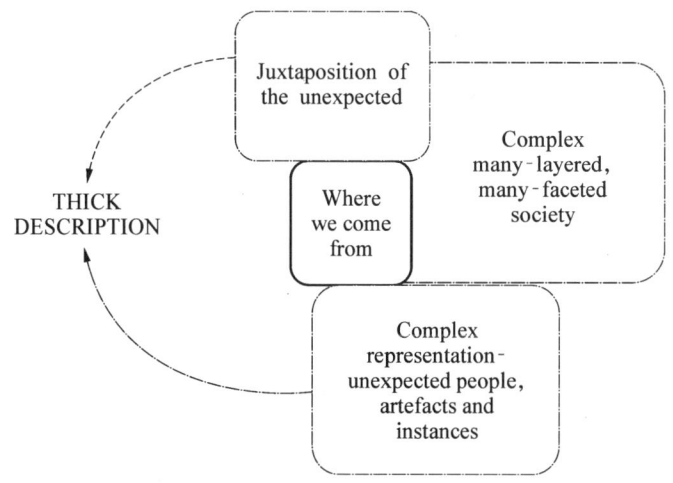

第五节 多角度了解信息和认知问题
Theme 5 Multi-perspective exploring and understanding

互动&体验 Interaction

1. Milanda 是个德国形体表演演员,她看上去很壮实,肌肉发达,因为需要承受很多高难度的表演动作,但她却说,"吃纯素是我们家的传统,我从小就不吃蛋、奶和任何肉类!"她的回答引来很多不同的反应,有人说她"撒谎",有人说她"不可思议",有人说她"一定偷偷在吃什么营养品",有人好心劝她"这样身体会垮掉的"。她为此颇有些烦恼。你的第一反应是什么?你可以用前面体验过的哪些跨文化技巧(放松、延迟判断、放入"不确定袋子"、多角度搜集信息等)来应对你的第一反应?

如果你的第一反应是"她撒谎",你可以＿＿＿＿＿＿＿＿＿＿＿＿＿＿＿＿＿＿＿＿
如果你的第一反应是"不可思议",你可以＿＿＿＿＿＿＿＿＿＿＿＿＿＿＿＿＿＿
如果你的第一反应是她"好可怜",你可以＿＿＿＿＿＿＿＿＿＿＿＿＿＿＿＿＿＿
如果你的第一反应是她"装逼",你可以＿＿＿＿＿＿＿＿＿＿＿＿＿＿＿＿＿＿＿

我们来试试"多角度认知"Milanda:

(1) 对 Milanda 做了进一步的观察,发现她更多的饮食细节,我们意识到,素食者里也有各自种不同的理解和行为:Milanda 的祖父、祖母、父亲和一个弟弟都是纯素食者,妈妈和哥哥不是;Milanda 自己从小就开始吃纯素;她并不介意同伴们烧肉食,也不介意桌上有肉食;她出门也从来不带自己的刀叉和调料;她吃葱姜蒜;她介意动物黄油;她从来没有想过吃素是高尚还是伪高尚,这就像她用左手还是右手写字一样自然而然。

(2) 我们问了问她表演团队里的朋友 Kara,平时都是怎么跟她一起吃饭的,Kara 这样说:一般来说我们没什么问题。她去我家里,我总是买好多蔬菜和素食快餐,准备豆浆和果汁。不过有时她还会因为烧菜用的是动物黄油而要求换盘,我觉得好尴尬。

(3) 我们从网络上总结了素食者吃素的一些原因,以及反对素食者的原因。

5.2 多角度认知问题
Understanding with multi-perspectives

支持的原因	反对的原因
从小看到小动物和家人的死亡过程	我也看过,怎么不像你那么矫情?
受到佛教对众生慈悲不杀生思想的影响	吃素食就不杀生了吗?植物也有感知系统。连石头都是有情众生。你不是还吃抗生素,用除菌洗衣液吗?
养殖畜牧业每年产生的温室气体排放量惊人	你不是也开车上班,坐飞机旅行吗?
现在的肉里有抗生素和激素	有很多素食者得贫血症和糖尿病。
这是更有格调的生活	你这是伪崇高!

4) 我们搜索了吃素行为的相关资料,

我们发现 _____ 也是吃素但很有力量的人;

我们发现吃素起源于 _____ ;

我们发现动物蛋白质对于人体是 _____ ;

我们发现 _____ ;

……

5) 我们通过这些学习和探究,有了对 Milanda 的素食行为"多角度认知",我们可以这样描述:

_____
_____
_____

你对身边某一位素食朋友的"多角度认知"是怎样的?

_____
_____
_____
_____

2. 我们对任何一个"他人",都可以尝试去"多角度认知",因为每个个体都是独特的,都有着自己的面貌和行动轨迹。我们可以用"ta 是怎样的一个日本人""ta 是怎样的一个素食者"、"ta 是怎样的一个基督徒"等,来真正去认识一个独特的日本人,一个独特的素食者,一个独特的基督徒。对于一个文化现象,我们也可以突破传统的认知,深入地、多角度地去描述它。试着去多角度地描述和认识下面的人和事:

● 一个童年在中国丹阳待过三年,小学在苏州,中学和大学在新西兰,在上海工作十年,住在美国十八年的人。

● 你的一个来自_____的_____。

● 你认识的一个_____岁来自_____的富二代。

第五节 多角度了解信息和认知问题
Theme 5 Multi-perspective exploring and understanding

3.关于"中国雾霾",我们可以做怎样的深度描述和多角度地评价?我们可以从以下这些角度来获取足够的信息帮助我们形成一个多角度的评价:
- 雾霾发生的不同地区
- 雾霾在不同地区发生的不同季节
- 各地雾霾发生的具体原因
- 中央治理雾霾的措施及其成效和限制
- 各地区治理雾霾的措施及其成效和限制
- 普通百姓的作为和不作为
- 媒体所带来的正面和负面影响
- 专家学者的研究和建议

1. Milanda is a German acrobatic artist. She looks strong and muscular because she has to bear a lot of difficult physical activities, but she said, "I am a vegan. My family has a vegan tradition. I've never had eggs, milk or any meat since I was a child!" Her answer provoked many different reactions. Some people said that she "lied"; some said she was "not believable"; others said she "must have been secretly consuming health products". Someone kindly warned her that "her body would be ruined" in that way. She is quite annoyed about this. What is your first reaction? What intercultural skills you experienced through previous themes (relaxation, delaying judgment, using "bag of uncertainty", exploring from multiple perspectives, etc.) can you adopt to deal with your first reaction?

If your first reaction is "she lied," you can_____

If your first reaction is "unbelievable", you can_____

If your first reaction is that she is "pathetic", you can_____

If your first reaction is that she "pretends to be special", you can_____

Let's try multi-perspective exploration about Milanda.

(1) Further observation of Milanda and more details of her diet show us that there are different understandings and behaviors among vegetarians and vegans. Milanda's grandparents, father and a younger brother are all vegans, while her mother and elder brother are not. Milanda has been a vegan since she was a child. She doesn't mind her companions cooking meat or putting meat on the table. She never goes out with her own knife, fork and seasoning. She eats onion, ginger and garlic. She dislikes animal butter. She never considers being

vegan is noble or not noble, but adopting it as naturally as she chooses to write with her left or right hand.

(2) We asked her friend Kara in the performance team about how they dine together. Kara said, "Generally speaking, we have no problem. When she comes to my place, I always buy a lot of vegetables and vegan snacks, prepare soy milk and juice. Sometimes she may ask for a clean plate because we use animal butter for cooking. I feel very embarrassed about that."

(3) By referring to the Internet, we have summarized some reasons for vegetarianism in general and some arguments for opposing it.

Reasons for supporting	Arguments for opposing
witnessing the death of small animals and family members at an early age	I have also seen it. Why am I not as emotional as you?
getting influenced by the Buddhist thought of compassion and no killing	Are you not killing as a vegetarian? Plants also have a perception system. Even the stones are sentient beings. Are you still taking antibiotics and using sterilizing laundry detergent?
huge annual greenhouse gas emissions from farming and animal husbandry	Don't you also drive to work and fly to travel?
There are antibiotics and hormones in the meat now.	There are many vegetarians who have anemia and diabetes.
This way of life is more stylish.	You are pretending to be noble!

(4) Let's keep exploring. Try to fill in the blanks with the information you found:

We found that some muscular actors or actresses such as_____ are also vegetarians;

We found that vegetarianism originated from

_____;

We found that animal protein means

_____to human body;

We found that _____;

...

...

...

(5) Through the exploring and inquiry, we have had a "multi-perspective understanding" of Milanda's vegan practice, which we can describe like this:

_____

_____

_____

第五节　多角度了解信息和认知问题
Theme 5　Multi-perspective exploring and understanding

What is your "multi-perspective understanding" of a vegan or vegetarian friend around you?

_____

_____

_____

2. We can try "multi-perspective understanding" for any "other person" because each individual is unique and has his own action track. We can truly know a unique Japanese, a unique vegetarian, or a unique Christian through questions like "What kind of Japanese is he/she", "What kind of vegetarian is he/she?", or "What kind of Christian is he/she?" For a cultural phenomenon, we can also break through the traditional cognition and describe it in depth and from multiple perspectives. Let's try to describe and understand the following people and things in multiple perspecitves:

● A person who has spent three years of childhood in Danyang, China, attended a primary school in Suzhou, went to middle school and university in New Zealand, worked for ten years in Shanghai, and lived for eighteen years in the United States.

● One of your female _____ from _____ .

● One _____ -year-old guy with rich parents from _____ .

3. What kind of thick description and multi-perspective description can we give to serious pollution problem in China called "Chinese Haze"? We can collect as much information as possible from the following perspectives:

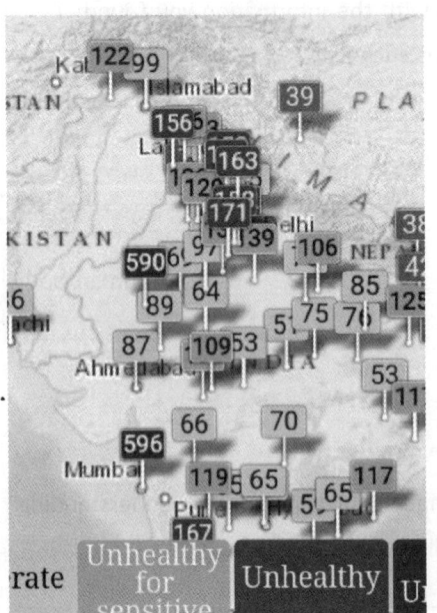

● Different seasons in which haze occurs in different regions

● The specific reasons for the occurrence of haze in different regions

● Measures for national governance of haze and their effectiveness and limitations

● Measures to control haze in regional governance and their effectiveness and limitations

● The actions and inactions of ordinary people

● Positive and negative impacts of the media

● Research and recommendations from experts and scholars

援引阅读 Quoted readings

"Whatever the origins, it is evident from German writers such as Gagel, Himmelmann, and writers such as Audigier, Duer et al. and Birzea at the Council of Europe, that democracy is the unquestioned value. The only questions are how to ensure that people understand and use their opportunities to behave democratically in public life.

This unquestioned assumption may be appropriate for North American and European societies, the societies for which these scholars are writing. American and European politicians also assume that democracy is the only form of politics that is valuable, to the extent that they are prepared to impose it on other countries. One of the issues that will arise from taking an intercultural perspective on citizenship is that even these assumptions should be questioned."(p.159)

——Byram, M. (2014). *From Foreign Language Education to Education for Intercultural Citizenship.* Shanghai: Shanghai Foreign Language Education Press.

"... A foreign language education perspective can complement and enrich this element of political education/'democratic learning', not only by providing the linguistic competence necessary to engage with people of other countries and languages in democratic processes but also, in the capacity for critical cultural awareness, by introducing a perspective of mediation and negotiation that does not presuppose democracy as the only source of values and governance."(p.165)

——Byram, M. (2014). *From Foreign Language Education to Education for Intercultural Citizenship.* Shanghai: Shanghai Foreign Language Education Press.

"The concept of culture, I espouse, and the whole utility the essays below attempt to demonstrate, is essentially a semiotic one. Believing, with Max Weber, that man is an animal suspended in webs of significance he himself has spun, I take culture to be those webs, and the analysis of it to be therefore not an experimental science in search of law but an interpretive one in search of meaning. It is explication I am after, construing social expressions on their surface enigmatical. But this pronouncement, a doctrine in a clause, demands itself some explication.

... Ryle's discussion of 'thick description' appears in two recent essays of his (now reprinted in the second volume of his *Collected Paper*) addressed to the general question of what, as he puts it, '*Le Pensuer*' is doing: 'Thinking and Reflecting' and 'The Thinking of Thoughts'."(p.20)

——Geertz, C. (2012). Thick description: Towards an interpretative theory of culture. In Chen, L. (Ed), *Culture, Cultures and Intercultural Communication: A Cross Disciplinary Reader*. Shanghai: Shanghai Foreign Language Education Press.

"全球文化正处于一个深刻的转型时期,国家汉学研究也不例外。

这种转型首先是出于普遍的文化自觉以及对人类现状的反思。……只有各民族充分的文化自觉,才能共同建立一个和平共处、各抒所长、共同发展的世界。因此,西方世界表现了对非西方文化、特别是中国文化的空前的关注。……另一方面,这种转型也关联于从二元对立思维方式向互动认知思维方式的转变。过去,'认知'所描述的是一个可信赖的主题去'认识'一个相对确定的客体,从而将其定义、划分、归类到已有的认识框架之中。互动认知的思维方式强调'他者原则',即从某一外在的参照物来重新认识自己;强调不确定的'互动原则',即强调主体和客体在认知过程中都有所改变……因此一切事物的意义并非一成不变,也不一定有预定答案,而是在千变万化的互动关系中,在不确定的无穷可能性中,有一种可能性由于种种机缘,变成了现实。"(第147-148页)

——乐黛云著.《跨越文化边界》.上海:东方出版中心.2012年.

"The principle of discovery is also implicit in thick description—seeing the complexity of a social event by looking at it from different aspects. The figure shows that the knowledge derived from understanding the juxtaposition of unexpectedness (for example, the woman in the film), complexity (for example, the layers in the film), and encounters with people, artifacts and instances [...] results in thick description. Thick description as a term comes from anthropology and qualitative research and involves two elements:

● deriving meaning from a broad view of social phenomena which pieces together different, interconnected perspectives.

● exploration, in which sense is made from an ongoing emergence of social phenomena, which may not immediately seem to connect, and which may indeed be unexpected."(p.8)

——Holliday, A., Kullman, J., & Hyde, M. (2017). *Intercultural Communication: An advanced Resource Book for Students*. Milton Park: Routledge.

第六节
移情与尊重

Theme 6
Empathy and respect

第六节 移情与尊重
Theme 6　Empathy and respect

6.1　体会移情
Experiencing empathy

 理论引介 Introduction

　　多渠道了解信息、多方面学习其它文化的具体内涵、多角度地思考和认识问题，为我们体会"移情"做了一些必要的准备。

　　"移情"这个词我们听到很多，为什么我们不断地提起它？它的内涵到底是什么？我们怎样才能真正做到？

　　"移情"最早是一个美学和心理学中的概念，后来被运用到语言学领域中。在跨文化交流研究中，这一技能在很多学者那里受到重视，得以讨论。INCA 研究报告(2004：4)对"移情"做出如下简要描述："(移情就是)你能够理解别人的想法和感受，见其所见，感其所感。这项跨文化技能除了需要你学习对方文化的知识和信息以外，还需要能感知别人的感受。它反映出你不愿意伤害人家的感情，也不侵犯人家的价值观念。"

　　移情基本包含四个方面：① 多方面地倾听和学习，深入认识对方的文化行为和观念；② 跟对方进行情感上的连接，在心理上能够"感同身受"，感受到对方的交流意愿、情绪、交流目的等；③ 理解和尊重对方的文化价值观念，不要试图说服或改变别人；④ 维护和保持自身文化观念的稳定。贝内特(2012)认为，同情是"想象把我们自己放在别人的体验里"，而移情是"想象我们的知性和感性都参与到别人的体验里"(142)。他分析说，同情来源于人类相似性假定和单一现实的理论，即相信人类在主要方面存在共性，表面差异只是一些"划痕"。其哲学根源是理想主义和经验论。移情则基于人类差异性假定和多元现实的存在，人们的指纹、脑波图形、基因密码等都不相同，个体之间存在各种差异，其哲学来源是相对论和系统论。(同上，2012：128-143)

　　这段话也即是说，同情是先假定大家是差不多的，因为他们没有和我们"相同"，才产生怜悯、为别人悲伤的感情，而移情是先假定大家是不同的，所以去体会和真正认可

6.1 体会移情
Experiencing empathy

他们的不同,承认别人虽然不同,但也是对的,最终尊重别人,不去改变别人。简言之,同情只是给予情感上的投影或施舍,而移情则是以不伤害别人感情为前提,"暂时地成为别人",努力参与到别人的意图和行为方式中,相信不同的方式可以达到同样的目的,或者相同的举动并不意味着相同的观念。比如,一个有"早鸟"习惯的妈妈在对待一个有"猫头鹰"生活节奏的孩子时,如果她有足够的移情技巧,她就可以比较轻松愉快地让孩子按照自己的节奏安排生活和学习;或者当你遇到一个不喜欢参加同学三十周年聚会的"老同学"时,能够充分参与到他所有的心理活动中,就不会埋怨他的行为是"怪异的"、"不可理喻的"、"骄傲无理的"、"不合群"的了。

By absorbing information from multiple sources, grasping the true meanings of other cultures in different aspects, and approaching problems from different perspectives, we are now ready to learn about and experience "empathy".

We have heard a lot about "empathy", but what is the true essence of "empathy"? How can we truly empathize others?

Originally used as an aesthetic and psychological concept, "empathy" was later introduced to linguistics. In intercultural communication studies, empathy, as a necessary skill for intercultural communication, has been highly valued by scholars and therefore received much attention. The INCA (Intercultural Competence Assessment Project, Assesse Manual, 2004: 4) describes empathy as follows: "You are able to understand other people's thoughts and feelings and see and feel a situation through their eyes. While this competence often draws on knowledge of how you would expect others to feel, it goes beyond awareness of facts. It often shows itself in a concern not to hurt others' feelings or infringe upon their system of values."

Empathy may be comprised of four parts: ① broadly listening to and learning from others so as to deepen the understanding of their cultural behaviors and values; ② emotionally bonding with and psychologically truly feeling others' wills and purposes of communication; ③ understanding and respecting others' cultural values instead of trying to persuade or change them; ④ guarding and maintaining the stability of one's own cultural values.

Milton Bennett (2013) believes that sympathy means "the imaginative placing of ourselves in another person's position" (211), while empathy means "the imaginative intellectual and emotional participation in another person's experience." (223) According to Bennett, sympathy derives from the human-similarity assumption and the one-reality theory, which holds that human beings are quite similar in

第六节 移情与尊重
Theme 6 Empathy and respect

major areas despite the "scratch"-like minor differences. While empathy, based on the human-difference assumption and the multiple-reality theory, underlines the individual differences such as in fingerprints, electroencephalogram, and genetic codes. (203 – 233)

Sympathy assumes that people are basically more or less the same. So when others fall into a sad situation, we produce a feeling of pity and sadness for them. Empathy, on the other hand, assumes that people are basically different in every sense, so we try to understand and recognize those differences without devaluing them. We learn to understand that although their values and behaviors are different from ours, they do have their own validities so we can't arbitrarily change their behaviors and thinking.

In short, sympathy means emotionally feeling or sharing other persons' sadness in their situation, while empathy means "temporarily becoming others" without injuring their emotions. Those who empathize with others try to engage themselves in others' will and behavior, believing that the goals can be reached in different ways, or the same action may contain different values. For example, an "early bird" mother with empathetic skills may happily accept her "night owl" child's living and learning style. Likewise, one will stop blaming his former classmate who refused to show up at the reunion to mark the 30th anniversary of graduation. By emphasizing with that absentee, he may well understand what his former classmate was feeling rather than criticizing him for his arrogance, and his asocial behavior.

思考 & 讨论 Reflection and discussion

1. 从你的生活经验、所学知识和常识来看,你更倾向于人和人之间更具相似性还是人类之间更具差异性? 理由是什么呢?

2. 当世界上许多国家以人道主义的方式接纳大量战争难民时,是基于同情还是基于移情?

3. 在跨文化交流中,移情是否比同情更能使交流过程和谐有效呢? 为什么?

1. According to your life experience, knowledge and common sense, which do you tend to believe in: there are more similarities among human beings or there are more differences among human beings? Why?

2. Many countries in the world accommodate in the name of humanitarianism large numbers of war refugees. Are they doing this for sympathy or for empathy?

3. What are the positive aspects of "sympathy"? In intercultural communication, will empathy do better than sympathy to promote the harmony and effectiveness? Give some reasons if you like.

6.1 体会移情 Experiencing empathy

学习者自己的提问和反思 Your own questions and reflections

1. _____
   _____
2. _____
   _____
3. _____
   _____

互动小锦囊 Toolkits for interaction

在这里我们推荐尝试 Bennett(2012:143 – 147)提出的培养移情力的六个步骤,归纳概括如下:

1. <u>假定差异性</u>:承认对方和我不同,而且是有道理的;认识到在不同的情境下我们对事物有不同的解读。
2. <u>了解自我</u>:充分了解自己的价值观念和思想,暂时地成为他人,并不意味着自我不可控制地丧失。
3. <u>搁置自我</u>:认识到自我,知道自我的边界在哪里,暂时让自己离开原有的环境,准备进入他人的领地。
4. <u>被引导的想象</u>:从他人的角度切入,想象他人的境遇和经历,就像参与一个戏剧或小说人物中一样。
5. <u>接受移情体验</u>:体会并接纳这种全新的、既熟悉又陌生的体验。
6. <u>重建自我</u>:体验过后还要记得回归自我,自我边界会得到调整和重建。

Here we recommend the six steps to develop empathy proposed by Milton Bennett. (2013: 226 – 230) They are summarized as follows:

Step 1: <u>Assuming Difference</u>: Acknowledge other people's differences from me and the significances of these differences. Realize that the same cultural phenomenon can be interpreted differently in different contexts.

Step 2: <u>Knowing Self</u>: Fully understand my own values and play others' part temporarily does not mean uncontrollably losing myself.

Step 3: <u>Suspending Self</u>: Being aware of "self" and its boundary makes it possible to temporarily leave my own territory and cross the boundary between other people and me.

Step 4: Allowing Guided Imagination: Imagine other people's circumstances and experiences from their perspectives, as if playing the part of a fictional character.

Step 5: Allowing Empathic Experience: Take and embrace such a brand new experience, which seems close or distant at times, as if entering someone else's body and world.

Step 6: Reestablishing Self: Remember to return to "self" after experiencing others' feelings. After the empathic experience, the boundary of self may be readjusted or rebuilt.

 互动&体验 Interaction

1. 我们先来做几个假定差异性的练习。你同意下面选项里的哪些说法呢？（可多选）。

■ 如果要获得优秀的高考成绩，
（A）可以在学校里跟着老师的要求和节奏学习和复习。
（B）可以不去学校上学，在家庭学校里读书和游学。
（C）在普通高中上学。
（D）在有较高一本达线率的重点高中学习。

■ 关于一个人身上的男性或女性特征，我认为：
（A）生理上是男性/女性，就是一个男性/女性。
（B）生理上是男性，心理上可能是女性。
（C）有些男人生理上是男性，心理和行为上可能比别的男性更多些"女性特质"，比如温和、细腻，容易伤感。
（D）有些由男性变性为女性的人，他们不应该再去男厕所或女厕所，而是应该去"变性人"厕所。

■ 对于改革开放后在美国生活的第一代和第二代移民，
（A）他们觉得总体上他们在美国的生活比当初在中国好。
（B）他们仍然对中国有着深厚的感情，希望中华民族富饶强大。
（C）其中在政界和经济界表现突出的华人领袖是美籍华裔中的精英，他们有素养，有能力，可以代表美籍华人们发声。
（D）他们应该作为"少数族裔"在美国政策中被作为一个整体来考虑。

2. 从下面角色里选取一个或几个来演一演，你可以发挥想象力，补充具体的情节：

- 一个小偷非常后悔偷了一个游客的钱包。
- 一个忙碌的老板不耐烦地在电话里拒绝听五岁的儿子唠叨学校的事情。
- 一个被嘲笑、被当猴看的外国游客。
- 一个唠唠叨叨的大学辅导员。
- 一个冷冰冰的超市收银员。

3. 去体验"移情",其实在现实生活中是非常难做到的:因为那有时就是要我们做自己不喜欢、不习惯做的那些事啊。比如,我们给闺蜜买礼物,自己不喜欢去买 LV 这些包包,但闺蜜就是心仪它们呢。你出国在外会为她牺牲自己的旅行时间而去商场为她代购吗?

还有这些情况,你可以试着去"参与"当事人的感情和认知(有些难度是吗?):

- <u>母女之间的相互移情体验</u>:我家娃的性观念非常开放,觉得性和情是两码事,她有各种"随意"的性行为,我跟她断绝母女关系了,根本就不是我女儿!
- <u>我与朋友的相互移情体验</u>:那个朋友被我屏蔽了,他整天晒、秀,极度张扬和油腻。
- <u>官员和村民的相互移情体验</u>:山区的发展,一定要改水、改厕,建学校,不要考虑村民的想法。他们不懂的。
- <u>我和老爸的相互移情体验</u>:我爸是大老板,家里很少见到他,去公司见他还要预约!哪里还当我是他儿子呢?
- <u>独立旅行者和中国旅行团的相互移情体验</u>:实在搞不懂这些跟团游的中国人,整天走马观花,疲于奔命,不懂旅行的真正意义!

这些情况,你觉得该怎样使用"移情"策略来缓解冲突?你可以在下面补充自己生活中的一些冲突的实例,然后可以重新思考改善这些冲突的可能性,比如用"想想在_____情况下,我也_____"来造句和体会移情:

- _____
- _____
- _____

1. Let's first do some exercises on "assuming difference". Which of the following will you choose to do? There might be more than one choice.

- If you want to get a high score in the College Entrance Examination (CEE), you can

(A) arrange your learning and review work according to teachers' requirements and schedules from school.

(B) choose homeschooling and study tours instead of going to a traditional school.

(C) go to an ordinary high school.

(D) go to a key high school with a relatively high top-university enrollment rate.

第六节 移情与尊重
Theme 6　Empathy and respect

■　About the masculine or the feminine characteristics of a person, I think:

(A) a person is a male/female as long as he/she is physically male or female.

(B) a person can be physically male and mentally female.

(C) some men are physically male but have more "feminine characteristics" than other men, such as mildness, meticulousness and sentimentality, in their psychology and behavior.

(D) transgender people should use neither men's nor women's toilets. Instead they should use the "transgender" toilets.

■　About the first and the second generations of Chinese immigrants to the USA after China's Reform and Opening-up Policy (This policy allows many Chinese to study in, work in or immigrate to other countries.) was launched:

(A) these people believe that their life now in the US is generally better than what life is like in China.

(B) these people still maintain deep patriotism and have hope for a prosperous and strong Chinese nation.

(C) these people who have become leaders in politics and economy are the elites of Chinese-Americans with high attainment and capability to speak for this group.

(D) these people should be regarded as a racial minority group in the US policy making.

2. Play one or several roles of the following list. Use your imagination to add specific details.

■　A thief who bitterly regrets stealing a purse from a tourist

■　A busy entrepreneur who impatiently interrupts his son's mumbling about what has happened at school

■　A foreign tourist who is laughed at because he looks "eccentric"

■　A college teacher who keeps urging and advising the students to make progress

■　A supermarket cashier who wears an expression of apathy

3. To empathize others is rather hard to manage in real life, for it sometimes means we have to do something we dislike or aren't used to. For example, we have to send our girlfriends Louis Vuitton handbags, the gifts they like, even though we don't like luxury bags at all. When you are traveling abroad, will you sacrifice your precious time to make purchases for your girlfriend/boyfriend?

In the following cases, you may try to "participate in" the emotion and perception of the roles. (Is that a bit difficult?)

■　<u>Experiencing empathy between the mother and the daughter</u>: "My daughter has a very liberal attitude towards sex and believes that sex and love can be separated. She has many casual sex relations. I have disowned her. She's not my daughter any more."

▍ <u>Experiencing empathy between me and my friend</u>: "I have blocked that friend on WhatsApp because he's so fond of showing off and appears rather boasting."

▍ <u>Experiencing empathy between the official and the villagers:</u> "To develop the mountainous regions, we have to rebuild the rural waterworks and latrines. Don't worry about how the villagers think, for they know nothing about it."

▍ <u>Experiencing empathy between me and my father</u>: "My father is a company president, and I can hardly see him at home. When I want to meet him at his company, I even have to make an appointment. Does he know I'm his son?"

▍ <u>Independent travelers from other countries and Chinese group travelers</u>: "I really don't understand these Chinese tour groups. Why do they travel in such a rush yet see little?"

In the cases above, how can the "empathy" strategy be used to ease the tensions? Please list some more conflicts you meet in life and reflect on the possibility of resolving them. You can make sentences as "I remember that when _____ I also _____" to help you to emphasize:

▍ _____
▍ _____
▍ _____

第六节 移情与尊重
Theme 6　Empathy and respect

6.2　真正做到尊重
Being truly respectful

 理论引介 Introduction

我们把尊重单独作为一个部分,是因为人们常常把它放在嘴边,但能做到真正尊重他人文化观念和文化习俗的人并不多见。到底什么是尊重?怎样做到真正尊重别人呢?

尊重看上去是一个比较宽泛、甚至空洞的字眼,但它其实来源于实实在在的技巧,只有在具体的跨文化技能上尽量做到位,尊重才会变成一个实在的、可以被感知的事物,它既是一种姿态、心态,也是一种认知和一种行为。Deardorff(2011)在给联合国教科文组织的工作报告中,把"尊重他人价值观"列为五个跨文化基本技能中的第一个。

真正的尊重,其来源是前面章节里所说的各种跨文化认知和技能,包括认识到文化的内部特质(如异质性、延展性、流动性)、培养进入"跨文化通道"的意识、放松心态、承认"不同但合理"、延迟判断、多多倾听和学习别人的文化内涵、体会移情等。在做到这些内容的过程中,"尊重"的意识和心态也就可以真正地培育起来了。

INCA 研究报告(Assessor Manual,2004:6-7)里这样描述"尊重他者":"认为别人的观念、习俗和日常行为虽然和你的不一样,但从他们的情境中去看是有价值的。你不一定认同他们的观念和习俗,但你强烈地意识到他们这样做具有合理性,是值得尊重的。因此当你有时在原则性问题上有不同看法时,既要坚定,又要有点外交策略。"

尊重不仅仅是礼貌地打招呼,或者给老人让座,或者不和老师争论问题。尊重是一种承认而不是否认,承认差异,承认相异的存在其背后的合理性,并由此而承认边界的存在。前面部分说的移情,它最终的外在表现,就是真正地尊重,只有真正体会到移情,才能做到真正地尊重别人。

6.2 真正做到尊重
Being truly respectful

We discuss "being respectful" in a separate part because people often mention it, but many actually fail to be respectful. So what is being respectul? How can we be truly respectful?

Respect seems like a general and even a bit empty word, but it actually comes from practical skills. Only if one copes well with intercultural communication skills can respect be something practical and perceptible. In short, it is an attitude, a mindset, a perception and a behavior. In a work report to the UNESCO by Darla K. Deardorff (2011), "being respectful to other people's values" ranks first in the five basic skills of intercultural communication.

True respect comes from the intercultural communication cognitions and skills discussed in the previous themes. They include: understanding the heterogeneity and the hybridity of culture, loosening up oneself, developing the awareness of entering the intercultural tunnel, delaying judgment, exploring with multiple-perspectives, truly understanding other cultures and empathizing. Only by applying all the above skills, can one truly cultivate the consciousness and skills of "being respectful".

According to a research report by INCA (Assessor Manual, 2004: 6-7) " respecting for otherness" means " you are ready to regard other people's values, customs and practices as worthwhile in their own right and not merely as different from the norm. While you may not share these values, customs and practices, you feel strongly that others are entitled to them and should not lose respect on account of them. You may sometimes need to adopt a firm but diplomatic stance over points of principle on which you disagree."

Respect is more than greeting others politely, offering your seat to the elderly, or avoiding arguments with your teachers or parents. It is an acknowledgement rather than a denial: acknowledging the existence and rationality of differences and thus acknowledging boundaries. The full expression of empathy, which has been discussed in the previous section, is being truly respectful to other people. Only by truly understanding the meaning of empathy can you be truly respectful to other people.

思考 & 讨论 Reflection and discussion

1. 你认可"对事不对人"这句话吗？为什么？
2. 海关可以采用开"海关锁"的方式打开旅行者的行李箱检查物品，这是不尊重个

第六节 移情与尊重
Theme 6　Empathy and respect

人隐私吗？

3. 当企业员工个人的民族习俗与公司文化发生冲突时，应该怎么办？

1. Do you agree with the statement, "just focus on the issue, not the person?"

2. The Customs officials sometimes use "customs locks" as a means to open and check through travelers' cases. Is this a violation of an individuals' privacy?

3. What should be done when an employee's own ethnic customs are in conflict with the company cultures?

学习者自己的提问和反思 Your own questions and reflections

1. _____

2. _____

3. _____

互动小锦囊 Toolkits for interaction

INCA 研究报告（Assessor Manual，2004：10）里，关于"移情"和"尊重他者"这两个技能分别有三个能力级别的描述。

	基本能力	中级能力	高级能力
移情	以好奇的眼光看待不同文化的外国人，对他们那些看上去很奇怪、陌生的行为和经历感到疑惑，但试着去"允许他们那么做"。	开始在脑海里列出一个"清单"，看看他人是怎样理解、感觉和应对一系列自己以为"常规"的情况。逐渐开始下意识地从他人的角度来认识事物。	将他人接纳为一个行为一致的个体，采取角色参与、放弃自我中心等技巧，能意识到不同视角的存在，在工作场合开展相关的交流与互动过程。
尊重他者	并不能时时意识到与别人的不同，即使意识到了，也不能区别自己的判断是否得体。当某种不同文化观念得到一致认可时，只能将就接纳，但尽可能少地接触和参与。	在日常生活里能够接受别人的价值观、习俗和行为没有什么好坏，但前提是不能违背自己的价值观。乐意去让他人感到舒适，不愿意冒犯他人。	尊重价值系统的多元性，对这些价值系统有思考有认知，从而在合作中保证平等待人。能够有策略地应对人与人之间不接纳而出现的伦理问题。

In INCA Assessor Manual (2004:10), "empathy" and "respect" can be described at three levels:

	Basic	Intermediate	Full
Empathy	Tends to see the cultural foreigner's differences as curious, and remains confused about the seemingly strange behaviours and their antecedents. Nonetheless tries to "make allowances".	Has the beginnings of a mental checklist of how others may perceive, feel and respond differently to, a range of routine circumstances. Tends increasingly to see things intuitively from the other's point of view.	Accepts the other as a coherent individual. Enlists role-taking and de-centring skills, and awareness of different perspectives, in optimising job-related communication/interaction with the cultural foreigner.
Respect for otherness	Is not always aware of difference and, when it is recognised, may not be able to defer evaluative judgement as good or bad. Where it is fully appreciated, adopts a tolerant stance and tries to adapt to low-involving demands of the foreign culture.	Accepts the other's values, norms and behaviours in everyday situations as neither good nor bad, provided that basic assumptions of his own culture have not been violated. Is motivated to put others at ease and avoid giving offence.	Out of respect for diversity in value systems, applies critical knowledge of such systems to ensure equal treatment of people in the workplace. Is able to cope tactfully with the ethical problems raised by personally unacceptable features of otherness.

互动&体验 Interaction

1. 中国人讲究"亲密无间",认为这是最能体现关系好的标志。闺蜜们可以睡一张床,共用化妆品,甚至彼此分享自己的收入状况和债务状况。兄弟们可以相互打抱不平,甚至两肋插刀。借了钱什么时候还是小事,不要丢了情分。而在有些注重个人隐私的观念里,这些做法就太没有"分寸"了。

想想你平时的行为,你和朋友、家人之间在哪些方面保留了分寸和界限呢?

你也可以和一些外国朋友们聊一聊,看看他们有没有界限。比较一下,你发现了什么?

2. 下面的对话是课堂老师和她的朋友关于东阳"童子尿煮鸡蛋"的。里面的人关于童子蛋都是怎么说的?他们对童子蛋的接纳程度是怎样的?(1:非常接受和认可。2:能够接受。3:觉得好玩,想知道。4:觉得不能理解。5:非常不接受,坚决不被同化。)我们来找一找。

老师的朋友(A):_____

老师(B):_____

东阳本地人:_____

东阳小媳妇:_____

小媳妇的老公公:_____

小媳妇的老公:_____

第六节　移情与尊重
Theme 6　Empathy and respect

小媳妇的小姑子：

A：下次你问问学生们童子尿煮蛋他们怎么看

B：哈哈

B：东阳的风俗

A：我有东阳媳妇的朋友

A：她应该吃过

B：不谈味道我自己接受童子尿煮蛋不接受活珠子

A：还有照片

A：我全删了

B：哈哈哈 太好玩！

B：看过一个视频记者调查东阳煮鸡蛋的当记者不容易哈哈哈哈

A：我说也掺杂在里面，用个挑去就好了

B：这…排泄器官不一样啊

A：恶习得很呐。。当街一盆煮，咕噜噜翻滚一股尿骚气。我小姑子吃了不起痱子，我捏着鼻子说：屎尿乃人体废渣废水，别吃，太恶了。。一那小媳妇说的

A：东阳人说煮尿蛋的味道是春天的味道，呕呕呕。。一又小媳妇说人家拒绝同化

A：我公公说：好食好食，都咸到蛋心里去了。。他说这句话我们在吃饭，而后我吐了。。一又转

A：我先生说：小时候被大人拦住，在桶里撒一泡尿给一块糖一又转

B：童子把尿，有准头吗

A：据说几岁就吃几个

A：冷了以后的一圈一圈白的

A：（ ）你回来汇报吧

A：我让她饶了我，她还在放。她公公说她没能像她老公那进进清华，就是没吃童子蛋

看完别人对于东阳童子蛋的讨论，你现在心里什么感觉？我们如何运用本节所了解的跨文化技能，去体会、理解、移情和尊重东阳的这个民间习俗？

3. 既尊重别人的价值观念又坚守自己的价值观念，是需要一些"外交"策略或者谈判技巧的。比如中国人经常被诟病，说他们在国外旅行时在公共场合大声喧哗，因为外国本土人在火车上或餐厅里都彬彬有礼，很少高声说话。而当你更多地在国外旅行时，你会发现，吵闹不堪的餐厅也有很多，来自世界各地高声喧哗的旅客也并不少见。我们

怎样来根据具体情境来调整我们的思维，并采取一些灵活的策略，从而既能更宽广地接纳来自世界各地（包括来自中国）的朋友的"大声说话"这个行为特征，同时又做到尊重他人、维护公共空间的良好秩序和环境呢？

1. Many Chinese people see "being close-knit or intimate", as a symbol of good relations. Girlfriends can share a bed, their make-up, or even information about their incomes and debts. Buddies can defend each other against injustices or help each other regardless of their own lives. Many Chinese think that it's no big deal when their friends pay back their money since friendship always comes first. However, in some cultural values that highlight idividualism, the above practices are rather inappropriate.

Between you and your friends and family, what are the areas where you have maintained the boundary of intimacy?

You may also chat with your friends at home and abroad and find out their boundaries of intimacy in their relationship with their friends and family. What have you discovered?

2. The following WeChat dialogue is between a teacher and her friend about "spring eggs hardboiled in little boys' urine", a popular dish in Dongyang City, East China's Zhejiang Province. Try to read the dialogue. What are the different attitudes between people in the dialogue towards the urine-boiled eggs? To what extent does each accept this kind of dish? You may mark as follows:

1: entirely accepts and approves of;

2: can accept;

3: feels interested and curious;

4: cannot understand;

5: strongly disapproves of and refuses to change his/her mind.

The teacher:

Friend of the teacher: _____

Local residents of Dongyang: _____

A young wife in Dongyang: _____

Father-in-law of the young wife: _____

Husband of the young wife: _____

Sister-in-law of the young wife: _____

Friend of the teacher: Ask your students next time what they think of "urine-boiled eggs".

Teacher: Haha!

Friend of the teacher: It's the local custom of Dongyang. I have a friend who married a man from Dongyang. She should have tried it.

Teahcer: Regardless of the taste, I myself can accept the urine-boiled eggs.

Friend of the teacher: I once saved some pictures of this kind of eggs but deleted them all!

Teacher: Sounds so interesting!

Friend of the teacher: I once watched a video about this customs. It is such a challenge for the interviewer in the video~ ~ According to that video, the shit is also mixed up in the urine sometimes. People just use chopsticks to pick it out.

Teacher: How could they mix up things from different places in the body!

Friend of the teacher: My friend just told me she finds it so disgusting. She sees people just boil them in the street, and the eggs were grunting with weird smell. Her sister-in-law told her that if people eat these eggs they would not have prickly heat in summer time.

Friend of the teacher: She also said the local Dongyang people find the smell of the urine-boiled eggs the "smell of the spring"! But she said she refused to be assimilated.

Friend of the teacher: She said while they were having supper, her father-in-law said, "good taste"! She was about to vomit at his words.

Friend of the teacher: Her husband told her when he was a little boy, he was stopped by the adults in the street to pee in a bucket and got a candy for that!

Teacher: Can he pee exactly into the bucket at so young age~ ~

Friend of the teacher: According to the local customs, kids should eat the same number of eggs as their age. When the eggs cool down, there is white foam around them.

She said her father-in-law believes that the reason why she couldn't go to top universities in China is that she had never had urine-boiled eggs as her husband had!

After reading this discussion from Dongyang, what do you think now? How can we use the intercultural communication skills we've learned in this chapter to see, understand, empathize with and respect the local custom of Dongyang?

3. Respecting other people's values while holding fast to one's own beliefs needs some "diplomatic" strategies and/or negotiating skills. For example, the Chinese tourists are often blamed for being too noisy in public areas abroad. As you visit more foreign countries, however, you will find that there are also noisy tourists from other places in the world, in the restaurants or on the trains. How can we readjust our mindset contextually and take flexible strategies to truly respect those "noisy" behaviors but at the same time maintain an orderly public environment?

第六节 移情与尊重
Theme 6 Empathy and respect

 **援引阅读 Quoted readings**

"接近**他人**,就是质疑我的自由、我之为生物的自发性、我对于物的统治,就是质疑这种'前冲之力'的自由、这种奔腾的激情,对于这种激情来说,什么都是允许的,甚至谋杀。'不可谋杀'勾画出**他人**出席于其中的面容,这一诫令将我的自由置于审判之下。于是,那对真理的自由依附,认识活动,那在笛卡尔看来于确实性中依附于某种清楚观念的自由意志,便寻求一种并不与这种清楚分明的观念本身之光辉相一致的理由。一种因其自身的清楚性而矗立起来的清楚观念,有赖于某种自由之——严格地说是——个人性的劳作;这种孤独的自由并不对其自己进行质疑,却可以最大限度地经受失败。唯有在道德中,这样的自由才被质疑。道德因此支配着真理的劳作。"(第 296 页)

——伊曼纽尔·列维纳斯著.朱刚译《总体与无限:论外在性》.北京:北京大学出版社,2016 年.

"The concept of 仁/ren generates the anthropocosmic world view presupposing the unity of humanity with Heaven, earth and the myriad things and at the same time necessitates a global ethic, which is built upon a commonly shared feeling such as empathy. This global ethic also serves as a global communicative or dialogic ethic, which in turn ensures true intercultural communication or dialogue that creates the possibility of an anthropocosmic community or what is called a community of shared future for mankind."(p.30)

——Jia, Y., et al. (2018). *Experiencing Global Intercultural Communication*. Beijing: Foreign Language Teaching and Research Press.

"Furthermore, the aspect of power is essential. There's no way we can work on intercultural competence without problematizing power. Because whatever we do on a daily basis... whatever we—I mean, whether it's things we say, the impressions that we're giving—is related to power relations between us and the other. I think it's urgent to move away from very individual approaches where, for example, I am going to assess your intercultural competence, so I'm going to give you an interview. Or, I am going to ask you to talk to someone. I am going to observe how you behave, and I'm going to give you a grade. No, that doesn't make sense. I mean, I think that most of us don't really have intercultural competence. Or sometimes we do, sometimes we don't. I would give a grade to people who are working together. That would still be unfair, because I'm here, taking part in the interaction by observing them. So, of course, I have an influence on what these people are doing."(p.18)

——Dervin, F. (2017). *Critical Interculturality: Lectures and Notes*. Newcastle: Cambridge Scholars.

皋陶曰:"都！亦行有九德。亦言其人有德,乃言曰:载采采。"

禹曰:"何？"

皋陶曰:"宽而栗,柔而立,愿而恭,乱而敬,扰而毅,直而温,简而廉,刚而塞,强而义。彰厥有常,吉哉！"

译文:

皋陶说:"考察一个人的品行有九种美德。考察他的言论,如果此人有德,就告诉他,开始做事情吧。"

大禹问:"何为九德？"

皋陶说:"宽大而又谨慎细致;性情温和而又有独立见解;敦厚老实而又端庄严肃;富有才能却又恭敬而不骄傲;柔和温顺而又刚毅果断;耿直而又温和;为人简朴而又廉政;刚正而充实;强悍而又有道义。常常彰显和表彰这九种德行,就会吉利。"(第14-15页)

——樊东译注.《尚书》(虞书·皋陶谟).上海:三联书店,2013年.

第七节
动态地建构文化,因地制宜解决问题

Theme 7
Culture construction and contextual problem-solving

第七节 动态地建构文化，因地制宜解决问题
Theme 7 Culture construction and contextual problem-solving

7.1 "建构"一种文化
"Constructing" a culture

 理论引介 Introduction

目前为止，我们已经讨论了不少跨文化交流的技巧，如放松——开放——暂停判断——适当地概括去消除偏见和歧视——学习对方的背景信息——移情尊重，等等。这样我们也已经逐渐看出第二节里描绘的"跨文化通道"的基本模型。这既是相对完整的一个过程，从长远看又具有开放的特性，没有绝对的结束，因为随着时间的推移，这些技巧仍在不断相互作用、补充、发展，每个参与交流的个体其价值观念在这个过程中多少会处于不断调整中。

于是，在不断调整自身文化观念、尊重和接纳其它文化观念的同时，我们就会再次印证前面章节所说的：一种文化是相对稳定的，可以是一种音乐形式、一个节日、一个风俗，但它同时也具有一定的相对性和延展性，会随着岁月的变迁在内容上发生变化。因此我们会说，一种文化也是不断"建构"和"生成"的。

学者们试图用各种概念去解释和规定文化的这两个维度。他们会用"结构"、"界限"、"概括性知识"、"刻板印象"、"相似趋同轴"（the axis of similarity and continuity）（见1.1）"本质"等来描述文化的稳定的这一维度，用"相对性"、"非本质"、"新产品"、"相异迷思轴"（the axis of difference and rapture）（见1.1）等来描述文化的延展性这一维度。在第1.2我们曾用"一个有着柔韧边界的云块"来模拟文化的这两个维度。

值得注意的是，文化的这两个维度在解决具体文化冲突时有时可能会出现矛盾的情况。比如，关于穆斯林妇女佩戴完全遮盖头部的"布卡"面罩（Burka）这个问题。一个一直佩戴这种面罩的妇女来到禁止佩戴它的法国，她到底是否应该拿下面罩呢？按照传统固定的文化习俗，她是必须佩戴的，而当今世界对妇女权利赋予日益增强，越来越多的人反对这项习俗，尤其是穿戴全身遮蔽的"布卡"，因此这项习俗也在发生动态的"生成"。各个国家对待穆斯林妇女佩戴完全遮盖头部的面罩的立场开始变得不尽相同，尤其是在同一个国家里，对待这个问题其实是随着时间在地点、范围和程度上不断变化的。有些佩戴"布卡"的穆斯林妇女可能会因此经历某种"矛盾"的时刻。

再如，目前中国舞台上出现了不少把芭蕾舞、现代舞植入昆曲或京剧的做法，在艺

术评论家当中引发争议。这种植入,到底是对传统的破坏还是对传统的创新?老艺术家们可能更多地看到传统精粹被破坏得不伦不类,年轻的艺术家们可能更多地看到时代的发展带来的观看预期。新老艺术家们之间到底该怎么对话和调适呢?

所以,我们虽然常常知道文化是不断发展变化的,但可能并没有把文化的发展和每个文化习俗、观点对固有边界突破的那些紧张而细微的时刻真正联系在一起。建构主义们提出,在具体文化冲突环境中,我们要打破固定的思维,依据具体的目的和需要,来判断一种文化形态的改变到底该在哪个维度上进行,是该继续保持还是该发生变化,该发生怎样的变化,等等。更为重要的是,我们需要找到灵活应对的解决方案,采取不同交流策略,形成一种只适合正在经历某个具体情境下文化冲突的某个个体、某两方或某个小团体的"第三文化",或独特的"小文化",即我们中国人常说的"因地制宜地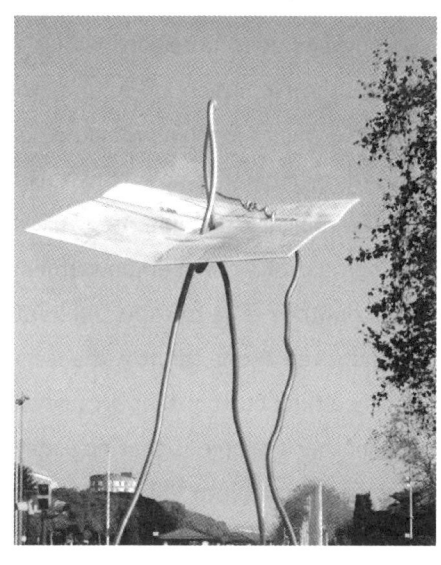
解决问题"。但这是需要长期的训练、并愿意付出相当的耐心和智慧的。有时,这个过程也需要克服极大的情绪障碍,才能冷静地分析状况,评估自己所采取的策略是否得当和有效。

We have already discussed several intercultural communication skills: relaxation, openness, delaying judgment, appropriate generalization to avoid prejudice and discrimination, collecting and learning about other cultures from multiple perspectives, empathy, and respect. From this process we can already see the basic shape of the "intercultural tunnel" as illustrated in Theme 2. The process in this tunnel is relatively and temporarily completed but over time these skills are further developing and mutually interacting with each other. The cultural understanding and behaviors of anyone who is passing through this tunnel are always open to adjustment and change. Therefore in the long run we find people's cultural values and customs are always extending and forming. So people are "constructing" a culture rather than "inheriting" a culture.

This means that while constantly readjusting our cultural values, and understanding and respecting others' cultural beliefs, we will find that although a culture is characterized by relatively stable artifacts such as a music type, a festival, or a tradition, it may also feature certain relativeness or tractility, undergoing changes as time goes by.

Scholars try to use different concepts to explain and define these two dimensions of culture. They tend to use "structure", "boundary", "general knowledge", "stereotype", "the axis of similarity and continuity" (See theme 1.1) and "essence" to describe the stable

第七节 动态地建构文化，因地制宜解决问题
Theme 7　Culture construction and contextual problem-solving

dimension of culture, while applying "relativeness", "non-essential", "novel product" and "the axis of difference and rapture" (See theme 1.1) to describe the dynamic dimension of culture. In theme 1.2, we use "a cultural cloud" to simulate the two dimensions of culture.

However, it is noteworthy that the two dimensions of culture may contradict each other in the resolution of cultural conflicts. Take Muslim women wearing a Burka as an example. When a Muslim woman who has been wearing Burka for her whole life comes to France, a country that now bans this custom on certain occasions, will she take the Burka off? According to the inherited, fix tradition, she must wear it. But nowadays with the development of women empowerment, more and more people start to oppose this custom. More countries start to show different attitudes towards it. If we take a closer look, we can find that even in one country, the laws on wearing Burka have changed or are changing now. So this cultural custom seems caught in dynamic contradictions.

Another example is that nowadays we see on stage that some ballet or modern dance has been injected into Chinese traditional operas such as Kunqu or Peking Opera. This has often aroused controversy among critics. It seems that some older artists feel the quintessence of Chinese culture has been destroyed, while some younger artists have keener eyes on the market needs that have been brought in by the new era. Is it possible to hold a dialogue between the old and the young artists?

Therefore, although we have always known that in general a culture is always developing, we haven't truly connected it with those tiny stressful moments when it finally breaks through its original fixed boundary. The constructionists thus propose that in the specific contexts of cultural conflicts, we should attend to the on-spot situation, its needs and demands, and then decide which direction that cultural custom or tradition should be emphasized. Should we firmly guard the traditions or should we change them to some extent? More importantly, we should break out of the fixed mindset to perhaps form a "third culture" or a "small culture", to put it simply, a creative and unique way that belongs only to an individual or the two sides or a small group of people who are undergoing cultural conflicts in a certain context.

We need to take a long-term training and be willing to employ great patience and wisdom if we want to find flexible solutions and different communicative strategies to help construct a "third culture" or a unique "small culture". Sometimes, we have to overcome huge emotional obstacles in the process so as to analyse the overall situation with a cool head and assess the appropriateness and the validity of the strategies taken.

思考 & 讨论 Reflection and discussion

1. 寻找灵活应对的解决方案,需要坚持自己的原则立场吗?
2. 两个不同的价值观念,是两个非此即彼的矛盾立场吗?
3. 文化具有生成性似乎并不难理解,但在我们灵活应对文化差异中它到底怎样起到作用呢?

1. Should we hold fast to our own principles while looking for flexible solutions?
2. Are the two different cultural values definitely contradictory to each other?
3. It is not difficult to understand that culture is a "forming" or a "constructing" process, yet what role does it really play if we flexibly deal with cultural differences?

学习者自己的提问和反思 Your own questions and reflections

1. _____
   _____
2. _____
   _____
3. _____
   _____

互动小锦囊 Toolkits for interaction

英国学者 Baker 在研究如何衡量"跨文化意识"的程度时列出了 3 个阶段 12 个方面的内容,它们都紧紧围绕"文化是处于流动、生成的状态"这个核心思想。(2012:66) 这三个阶段的主要内容概括如下:

第一阶段:基本的文化意识

在这个阶段,人们意识到文化是一整套大家公认的行为、信念和价值观;文化和情境会在人们对一件事情进行解释时起到作用;我们自身和别人都携带着由各自文化产生的行为、价值观和信仰,我们具有表达这些东西和比较这些东西的能力。

第二阶段:高级文化意识

在这个阶段,人们意识到文化习俗具有相对性;文化观念是暂时的,可以不断修正;在任何一个文化团体内都具有多种声音和角度;不同文化具有共同的认知地带,但也可能同时出现误解和交流失误。

第七节 动态地建构文化,因地制宜解决问题
Theme 7 Culture construction and contextual problem-solving

第三阶段:跨文化意识

在这个阶段,人们意识到跨文化时的参照、文化形式和交流行为不但与双方的文化背景相关,而且具有即时发生的情境和流动特征;文化刻板印象或概括性知识可以作为交流的起点,但要有能力超越它们;人们应有能力对各种文化模式、框架和参照等,进行协商和调适。

In his study on how to measure the different degrees of "(inter)cultural awareness", William Baker (2012: 66) lists 12 components in three levels, one important theme of which is the clear awareness that culture is fluid, hybrid, emergent, thus a process of constructing. Here is a brief summary of the main contents of the 12 components:

Level 1: Basic cultural awareness

At this level people are aware of the role culture and context play in any interpretation of meaning, and are aware of both our own and others' culturally induced behaviour, values, and beliefs. People have the ability to articulate them and to compare them.

Level 2: Advanced cultural awareness

At this level people are aware of the relative and open nature of cultural norms; and of the multiple voices or perspectives within any cultural grouping; and of the common ground between specific cultures as well as of possibilities for mismatch and miscommunication between specific cultures.

Level 3: Intercultural awareness

At this level people are aware that culturally based frames of reference, forms, and communicative practices are related both to specific cultures and also as emergent and hybrid, and that initial interaction are possibly based on cultural stereotypes or generalizations but are able to move beyond these through. People are able to negotiate and mediate between different emergent socioculturally grounded communication modes and frames of reference.

 互动&体验 Interaction

1. 很多人认可"我们的文化行为、价值观和信仰不是与生俱来的,而是习得而来的"这个观点。举我们对友情的理解为例。你心中的友情是怎样的?你是否愿意仔细回想一下,你心中这些对于友情的标准、理解、想象,是你什么时候、从哪里获得的?朋友?同事?书本?电影?中学?大学?然后,可否和你心目中认定的那个"好朋友"聊一聊,看看ta对友情的想法是不是完全和你一样。

2. 我们虽然一直在强调维护和秉承中国的传统文化,可是我们还是能找到很多中国的传统文化形式在漫漫岁月长河中不断演变发展的例子,比如剪纸和过年。通过网络我们查找一个我们喜欢的中国民间风俗不断变化的细节资料,并分享给朋友们或同学们。

3. 有新锐导演尝试改革中国的传统戏曲,让中国戏曲走向世界,在昆曲《桃花扇》演出中融入芭蕾舞表演,并在纽约上演,获得褒贬不一的评价。如果"根据具体交流的目的和需求灵活地寻求调适方案"来考察一个文化交流现象,我们怎么来分析这件事?

1. Many people believe that our cultural behaviors, values, and beliefs are not inherited but acquired and learned. Take our understanding of friendship as an example. What is it like in your mind? If you want, you can reflect on your own standards, understanding, and imagination of friendship. When and where did you get them? Were they from your friends, colleagues, books, movies, high school, or college education? You may also talk about it with your "best friend" and see if he or she thinks of friendship exactly the same way as you do.

2. Although we have been emphasizing the preservation and inheritance of the traditional Chinese culture, we can find a great many examples of traditional Chinese cultural forms undergoing constant changes throughout history, such as paper cutting and celebration of the Spring Festival. Please surf the Internet to find some detailed information about the "constructing" of one Chinese folk custom you like, and share your findings with friends or classmates.

3. There are avant-garde directors who'd like to adapt traditional Chinese operas to the global stage. They integrated ballet into the Kunqu opera performance *The Peach Blossom Fan* in New York and got mixed reviews. If we examine an intercultural phenomenon by following the rule of "flexibly readjusting solutions according to the specific purposes and demands of communication in a specific context", how could we analyze this incident?

第七节 动态地建构文化，因地制宜解决问题
Theme 7　Culture construction and contextual problem-solving

7.2　因地制宜解决问题
Solving the problems contextually

因地制宜采用方案和策略，来解决跨文化通道中遭遇的问题，会受到各种条件的制约。比如交流者本人的性格，天性豁达、直爽、不在乎的人，就可能话多些；而有的人害羞，稳重，不喜欢多说话；有的人在某些情境下在意别人对自己身份、地位的尊重，另一些时候就放松很多；有的人信仰坚定，不轻易动摇。采取灵活机动的策略似乎还受限于周遭环境的压力（比如跟上级交流）、占主导地位文化的压力（比如新移民）等，使人们在交流中处于弱势，不得不去痛苦地单方面调适自己的言行和思维，从而能够生存和融入。

学者 Kim（2014：98-99）归纳了五个影响和限制跨文化交流策略选择的因素，即 ① 是否清晰地表达了交流目的；② 最低程度地逼迫对方；③ 照顾对方的感受；④ 避免对方形成对"我"的负面评价；⑤ 顾及沟通效果。但有时交流者并不能很好地处理这五个方面，尤其不能平衡好自己的需求和对方的感受。

但这些因素并不真正影响跨文化调适过程和结果，也就是说，无论你是否是个开放的人，或者你无论遇到各种有压力的交际环境，你其实依然可以在某种程度上穿过"跨文化通道"，达到自己的交流目的，或让自己更加舒适。

在灵活地解决矛盾和冲突过程中，我们可以参考美国学者 Fisher 和 Ury（2012）关于"谈判"的详细探讨和他们给出的具体而有效的操作步骤。这些步骤基本适用于各种场合，如商业谈判、家庭纠纷、日常买卖、工作配合，甚至包括国家间的谈判，当然也包括文化冲突方面的调适。他们最核心的观点是，在各类谈判（根据具体情况寻求解决方案来调和矛盾）中，人们暂时不要聚焦于各自的立场和原则，而是要谋求共同的利益，发明互惠共赢的方案出来。人们发生矛盾的焦点，有时并不是方向和目的上的水火不容，而只是具体做法上的不同。同时，他们还积极地认为，对于强权的一方，或者是逃避不谈，甚至不按规矩出牌的对方，我们仍然有很多办法应对他们。

立场的坚持和冲突只是以语言或行为表现出的表面形象，真正冲突的是背后的原因，如经济上的损失、对别人的承诺、担忧失去安全感、失去控制权、失去身份感、身体健康方面的需求等。满足这些背后的愿望和要求，才是我们需要共同努力的方向。我们来看看下面这个表中的例子，也可以试着填上自己生活中的内容并看看能否解决。

7.2 因地制宜解决问题
Solving the problems contextually

冲突事件	表面立场	实际的问题和需求	解决方式	被满足的需求
王先生和王太太总是为不能一起好好吃早餐而争执。	王先生经常不在家吃早餐,说时间紧,来不及。	王先生单身久了,喜欢各种街边"早餐"的口味,不习惯被家庭生活束缚。	1. 准备些先生单身时喜欢的街边早点,加上太太的"特制"早点。 2. 夫妻有时(不用每天)共进早餐。	不被束缚的感觉,保持原有的早餐内容。
	王太太希望先生每天能吃完早饭去上班,说身体健康很重要。	王太太关心先生身体,也想和先生多些相处时间,认为早餐是一种有意义的"仪式"。		照顾先生的饮食起居,和先生温馨相处。

In contextually solving the problems in the intercultural tunnel, it seems that we are limited by various factors such as the characters of the communicators. Those who are extroverted tend to be more active in communicating with others, while those who are introverted are less willing to speak out. Some people care much about others' respect for their identity and status in certain contexts, while on other occasions they are far more relaxed. Some people look "stubborn", "too confident", "too much of ego", "very strong-willed" so that they "will never give in or surrender". Adopting flexible solutions may also be limited by the pressure from the surroundings (e.g., this can occur while talking to a superior), or from the dominant culture (e.g., this may be imposed on new immigrants); therefore, they may feel pressured into a position where they have to bitterly readjust their own behaviors and mindsets in order to survive or maintain the relationship.

Min-Sun Kim (2014: 98–99) summarizes five cultural-based conversational constraints: ① Clarity. ② Minimizing imposition. ③ Consideration for other's feelings. ④ Risking disapproval for self. ⑤ Effectiveness. Many communicators fail to break through these constraints, especially fail to balance their own needs and those of other people's feelings.

However, all these factors cannot truly affect the process and the result of intercultural readjustment. In other words, whether you are open-minded, or whether you feel pressured by the communicative environment, you can still, to some extent, get through the "intercultural tunnel" and reach your purpose of communication, or simply make yourself more comfortable.

In flexibly resolving contradictions and conflicts, we can refer to the detailed exploration of "negotiation" by Roger Fisher and William Ury (2012). The specific and effective methods they have offered can be generally applied in different contexts such as business negotiations, family disputes, business operations, workplace cooperation, and even international negotiations. The key point of the two scholars is that in different types of negotiations (i.e., looking for solutions to tackle contradictions in specific contexts) people should not focus on their own positions. Rather, they should seek a common ground and

Theme 7 Culture construction and contextual problem-solving

devise creatively win-win solutions. What people disagree upon is often the methods taken rather than the direction or the purpose of doing something. In addition, the two scholars also hopefully provide ways to deal with the powerful or the evasive and unpredictable side.

Holding fast to one's position and causing conflict that follows only show the direct demands through words or behaviors. True conflicts, however, always concern underlying causes such as financial loss, promises made to others, worries about insecurity, loss of control, loss of identity and physical or health needs. To satisfy these desires and demands is the shared purpose of us all and the direction we should really work to during the negotiation. Let's see the following example:

	Position on the surface	Actual problems and needs	Possible solutions	Needs that are met
Mr. and Mrs. Wang have always been arguing about having breakfast together.	Mr. Wang seldom has breakfast at home, saying he has no time for that.	Having been single for a long time, Mr. Wang prefers the "street breakfast" and finds the family life too restrained.	Prepare some "street breakfast" for Mr. Wang plus some "specialty" made by Mrs. Wang. They can sometimes, but not always, have breakfast together.	Mr. Wang can Keep to feel "free" and continue to have the street breakfast he likes.
	Mrs. Wang hopes her husband can have healthy breakfast at home together with her.	Mrs. Wang cares about her husband's health and regards breakfast as an important ritual in family life, a symbol of mutual love.		Mrs. Wang can take good care of her husband and enjoy the sweet moments of being together.

思考 & 讨论 Reflection and discussion

1. 一个智慧的、充满创造力的、可以谋求双方利益的谈判解决方案,有没有什么情况下就变得完全不可能?
2. 我们是否应该平衡谈判愿望和谈判所付出的代价?
3. 谈判时我们该如何对待自己的"底线"或"原则"?

1. In what context will a wise, creative and win-win approach to negotiation become invalid?
2. Should we balance the will to negotiate and the price to be paid for doing it?
3. How should we deal with our own bottom line or principle during a negotiation?

学习者自己的提问和反思 Your own questions and reflections

1. _____
_____

2. _____

3. _____

互动小锦囊 Toolkits for interaction

Fisher 和 Ury(2012:13)突破了一味妥协或一味坚持原则等传统的谈判思路,转而提出四个新的谈判策略。

解决问题的关键:	转变游戏思路——让谈判聚焦于给大家带来益处。
基本原则:	谈判参与方都是问题的解决者。谈判目的是通过有效、友善的方式寻求一个聪明的解决方案。
谈判策略1:对事不对人。	对人友善,对问题坚持,避免仅仅用对人信任来处理问题。
谈判策略2:聚焦于共同的利益而不是各自的立场。	发掘双方的利益所在。谨慎坚持所谓的"底线"。
谈判策略3:创想出几种互惠共赢的方案供选择。	创想出几种可选择的方案,随后再决定使用哪个。
谈判策略4:坚持使用客观的标准。	在一个客观标准之下,撇开双方的主观意愿来寻求解决方案。给出各自的理由,不要屈服于压力,而是受约于标准本身。

By breaking the traditional negotiating thinking of either simply compromising or simply adhering to principles, Roger Fisher and William Ury (2012:13) propose four new strategies for negotiation.

Solution	Change the game—negotiate on the merits
Principle	Participants are problem-solvers. The goal is a wise outcome reached efficiently and amicably.
Method 1: Separate the people from the problem.	Be soft on the people, hard on the problem. Proceed independent of trust.
Method 2: Focus on interests, not positions.	Explore interests. Avoid having a bottom line.
Method 3: Invent options for mutual gain.	Develop multiple options to choose from; decide later.
Method 4: Insist on using objective criteria.	Try to reach a result based on standards independent of will. Reason and be open to reason; yield to principle, not pressure.

第七节 动态地建构文化,因地制宜解决问题
Theme 7 Culture construction and contextual problem-solving

互动&体验 Interaction

1. 一个文化可以部分突破原有的价值观念,逐步或暂时和别的文化产生某种连接甚至融合,或者生成当时情境中一个新的文化形态。因此在处理具体的跨文化不适情况时,我们可以利用文化的这一特性来灵活地调适我们的心态和决策。下面这个情况下,你会怎么办?

按照中国传统欣赏京剧的做法,遇到精彩表演时,是要"叫好"的,但按照西方欣赏交响乐的礼仪,只能在结束时热烈地鼓掌。那么,当一个中国京剧迷正在伦敦一家音乐厅里听"京剧交响乐"时,遇到一段精彩的表演,是该叫好、鼓掌还是不该这么做?如果有外国人阻止他喝彩,他该怎么办?争吵?辩驳?不再发出任何声音?

2. 下面这些一开始看上去"不可能完成的任务",实际上却可能在某种程度上通过沟通和谈判得到解决或缓解,但我们首先要先从分析冲突双方的立场及其背后双方的实际利益需求开始。

情况一:某大四学生(A)一门期末考试不及格,任课老师(B)要该生参加补考。该学生已经申请国外大学研究生,毕业前成绩册里不能有挂科和补考成绩。

A方立场	A方实际利益和需求	B方立场	B方实际利益和需求

情况二:某年轻打工码农(A)看中一套地点合适、装修较好的两室一厅,需要两千元一个月的租金,他需要一间房间编程,一间和女朋友共住,但他和女朋友每月租房预算一共只有一千元,房东(B)说:"你开什么玩笑!"

A方立场	A方实际利益和需求	B方立场	B方实际利益和需求

情况三:一个全球石油公司法国办事处的主任(A)对一个从中东办公室刚调来的女下属(B)说:"我知道你需要这份工作,我们也知道目前只有你能做这个工作,我们很

7.2 因地制宜解决问题
Solving the problems contextually

需要你来这里帮忙三个月,但我们国家是禁止戴 Burka(一些穆斯林妇女佩戴的遮住全部头部的面罩)的,请你这三个月内要解下来。"

A方立场	A方实际利益和需求	B方立场	B方实际利益和需求

3. 五年前,中国女孩美惠硕士毕业了,她和同一个专业的法国小伙 Jacob 已经谈了三年的恋爱。于是,她跟 Jacob 沟通了好几次准备结婚的事情,但发现 Jacob 并没有结婚的打算,而且态度很坚决。他只希望和她认真地生活在一起,没有钻戒,没有任何的仪式,包括结婚。当时,她很伤心,跟父母和在美国的闺蜜说了这件事。

父母非常生气,说这样的人,不负责任,趁早分手。但她在美国的闺蜜却跟她说,自己很多朋友有固定长期的生活伴侣(partner),有的在一起生活了二三十年了,但都拒绝走进婚姻。而且,各自都有自己的朋友圈,出门旅行也是和朋友一起。兄弟姐妹间同处一城,几年也不见面。"我觉得他们有意无意在保持和最亲密人的距离,"她说。美惠发现,同样的话 Jacob 基本都跟她说过。

美惠不愿意就这样离开 Jacob,因为除了他们两个在专业上有着共同的事业和话题,她在他那里还感受到从来没有过的真诚和爱意。

请试着帮美惠和 Jacob 完成下面这些做法:

(1) 将矛盾焦点从双方各自一次性提出的强硬条件/底线/立场,转移到双方共同的需求上,美惠原有的"底线"是 _____,Jacob 原有的"底线"是 _____。

(2) 两个人好好聊一聊,将分歧归结为文化上的差异,因为 _____
_____
_____。

(3) 美惠试着告诉 Jacob 她自己需要婚姻的真正需求和目的是:_____
_____。

(4) Jacob 试着和美惠一起分析出他不愿意结婚背后真正的需求和理由:_____
_____。

(5) 两个人找出几种基本满足双方需求的可行的解决方案:

■ _____

■ _____

■ _____

……

第七节 动态地建构文化，因地制宜解决问题
Theme 7 Culture construction and contextual problem-solving

1. A culture can partly break out of its existing boundary and gradually or temporarily get connected to or even partly integrated into another culture, or just form a "small culture" in a unique context. Therefore, while handling specific intercultural tensions, we may use this nature of culture to flexibly readjust our mindset and decision-making. In the following situation, what will you do?

According to Chinese traditions, the audience would shout something like "bravo!" to the performer along with the process of an excellent performance in the Peking Opera show house. But according to the etiquette of appreciating symphony, people are supposed to keep quite during the whole show and shout "bravo!" only when the excellent performance is fully over. If a Chinese Peking Opera fan is now enjoying a performance of "Peking Opera Symphony" (a symphony concert combined with Peking Opera show) in a concert hall in London, should he applaud and shout "bravo" or not? If some foreign audience prevent him from making any noise, what will he do?

2. The following cases of "mission impossible" can actually be completed to some degree through communication and negotiation, but we should first start from analyzing the bottom lines/positions and the true needs of the two parties.

Case 1: A senior college student (A) is failed by his professor (B) in the final exam and is demanded to take the resit. The student has already applied for an overseas postgraduate school, which requires no failed subject or resit records in the undergraduate transcript.

A's position	A's true interests/demands	B's position	B's true interests/demands

Case 2: A young software programmer (A) intends to rent an ideally-located and well-decorated apartment with two rooms and one sitting room, with a monthly renting fee of 2,000 Yuan. He plans to use one room as his programming workshop and one to live with his girlfriend. However, he and his girlfriend have just a monthly rent budget of 1,000 Yuan. The landlord (B) sneers, "Are you joking?"

A's position	A's true interests/demands	B's position	B's true interests/demands

Case 3: The director of the French branch office of a global oil company (A) says to a female staff recently transferred from the Middle-East branch office (B), "I know you need

this job, and we know you are the only capable candidate now. We sincerely hope that you can help us for three months, but since it is forbidden to wear Burka in our country, please take it off during your work here."

A's position	A's true interests/demands	B's position	B's true interests/demands

3. Five years ago, Meihui, a Chinese girl got her master's degree in a university in France. She had been in love with a French young man named Jacob for three years. Meihui talked to Jacob several times about getting married, but found that he had no plan for that and insisted on just living with her. There would be no diamond ring, no ceremony, and no marriage. Meihui felt heartbroken and told her parents and an American girlfriend about her situation.

Meihui's parents were so irritated that they urged her to break up with Jacob as soon as possible, but her American girlfriend told her that she has some friends who have long-term life partners and reject marriage after living together for 2 to 3 decades. The couples have their own respective social circle and are fond of traveling with their own friends. "I think they are consciously or unconsciously maintaining the distance with those close to them," she said. Meihui found that Jacob had told her the same thing.

Meihui would not break up with Jacob, because they share many common values in life and common pursuits in career. Besides, Jacob has given her the love and warmth she'd never experienced before.

Please try to complete the following steps for Meihui and Jacob to negotiate on this issue.

(1) Shift the focus of contradiction from each side's directly stated bottom line/position to the shared demands. The original bottom line of Meihui is _____ _____, while that of Jacob is _____ _____.

(2) After a good talk, Meihui and Jacob attribute their dispute to cultural differences, because _____ _____ _____.

(3) Meihui attempts to tell Jacob the true cultural demands and reasons for her insistence on marriage. _____ _____.

(4) Jacob attempts to work with Meihui to analyse the true demands and reasons for

第七节 动态地建构文化,因地制宜解决问题
Theme 7 Culture construction and contextual problem-solving

his unwillingness to get married. _____
_____.

(5) The couple work out several workable solutions that can generally satisfy each other's demands.

- _____
  _____
- _____
  _____
- _____
  _____

......

7.2 因地制宜解决问题
Solving the problems contextually

援引阅读 Quoted readings

"This is why I have preferred, in the course of my open work-in-progress between China and Europe, to deal with *divergences* rather than differences. Because divergence (*écart*) promotes a point of view which is no longer that of identification, in favour of what I will call exploration: it envisages the extent to which various possibilities can be deployed and what intersections are discernable in thought... *to what extent*, in China or in Greece, on one front or another, dealing with them in one way or another, can the frontiers of what is thinkable be discerned and, more than this, can an inkling of what one has not thought to think be ventured?"(p.26)

——Jullien, F. (2011). Trans. Richardson, M. & Fijalkowski, K. *The Silent Transformations*. Calcutta: Seagull Books.

"文化认同的延伸则由两个互为表里、相辅相成的向度构成：其一是面向独特性延伸；其二是面向普遍性延伸。朝着独特性方向延展，意味着亚文化群体或个人的特性与行为方式不断被吸纳与整合进来，文化认同对群体内部成员变得更为多元与包容。文化认同的本质体现在主体间性（intersubjectivity）——通过社会个体相互交流、相互沟通而形成的集体共识。面向独特性延展过程，交际者与文化群体内部成员反复、耐心商讨，把那些得到普遍赞同与欣赏的亚文化以及个体的言行与观念吸收进来，为原有文化认同增添新元素，使其内容更多样。（……）

面向普遍性拓展之时，交际者跨越文化边界，亲身体验新的文化。他们一方面虚心学习新的文化知识、充实自己，另一方面向其它文化的成员介绍自己的文化，让他人了解自我，努力商讨跨文化协议。经过双向延展，交际者文化认同的内涵愈益丰富，身份定位更趋开放、灵活，他们的思想观念与行为方式开始具备较高的跨文化可比性与通约性。交际者因此获得整合不同文化视角，在互动中进行反思和自我转变的能力。"（第148页）

——戴晓东.《解读跨文化认同的四种视角》.《学术研究》.2013年第9期，144-151页.

"我执的基本目的就是要保持身份认同，但是在一个变化多端和复杂的世界里，我们又能保住些什么呢？我们的念头和情绪都是持续在改变的，在这样快速变化的情况之下，我们很难保持从容，我们很快就会感到失落。

当我们的内在被动摇，我们不知道要怎么办，也找不到归属感，所有的人、事、物似乎都在威胁着我们。这个混乱是由我执制造出来的，唯一的方法就是从这样的混乱及复杂中转身离开，如此我们才能发现真正的自己！"（第116-117页）

——吉噶·康楚仁波切著.丁乃竺译.《无我的智慧》.西安：陕西师范大学出版总社

第七节 动态地建构文化,因地制宜解决问题
Theme 7 Culture construction and contextual problem-solving

有限公司,2010年.

　　"批评往往暗含着期待。对他人的批评实际上间接表达了我们尚未满足的需要。如果一个人说'你从不理解我',他实际上是渴望得到理解。如果太太说'这个星期你每天都工作到很晚,你喜欢工作,不喜欢我',那反映了她看重亲密关系。

　　如果我们通过批评来提出主张,人们的反应常常是申辩或反击。反之,如果我们直接说出需要,其他人就较有可能做出积极的回应。"(第50-51)
　　　　——马歇尔·卢森堡著.阮胤华译.《非暴力沟通》.北京:华夏出版社,2018年.

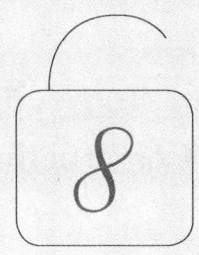

第八节
动态的文化身份和柔韧的文化疆界

Theme 8
Dynamic cultural identities and pliable cultural boundaries

第八节　动态的文化身份和柔韧的文化疆界
Theme 8　Dynamic cultural identities and pliable cultural boundaries

8.1　动态地建构和调适文化身份
Constructing and adjusting cultural identities dynamically

 理论引介 Introduction

我们很难想象,一些在美国居住了近三十年的第一代华裔移民,回中国探亲访友时,会有一种不适感和焦虑的心情。其中一位美籍华裔女士这么说道:每次我回国时给国内的亲朋好友带礼物都是一件头疼的事。带点美国的特色吧,他们说你显摆;带点一般的东西吧,他们说国内现在发展很快,什么没有,以为我们还生活在三十年前啊?而且其实国内的朋友们还是比较看重东西的价值,我在美国就没有这些担忧,朋友们都喜欢特别的、有真正心意的礼物,并不在乎礼物的价值有多少。感觉我回中国每次都搞不清楚自己到底是谁,不知道该带什么礼物。

其实,这位美籍华裔女士正处在暂时的文化身份认同的困惑中。文化身份认同过程中人们常常会问,我是谁,我到底属于哪里,哪个团体,哪个单位,哪个组织,哪个阶层,等等。文化身份/认同是近二三十年来越来越受到学者关注的重要概念,它更多地属于社会心理学或社会文化学的范畴,但语言学领域也逐渐在探讨这个概念。

随着全球化的发展,各种文化混搭(cultural mixing)现象时有发生。人们的流动性增加后,身份的变化和焦虑也随之而来。在不同的文化混搭情境中,人们会采取不同的文化身份认同模式。融合性较强的认同模式包括"整合"(integration),即将两种或两种以上的认同合二为一,既认可这样,也认可那样;"转换"(alternation),即在不同的领域使用不同的策略;"协同"(synergy),即指一个人在不同文化的冲击下,构建出一种不同于几种文化简单叠加或并列的新的身份认同。(吴莹:2016)

身份认同的相关理论目前有身份管理理论(Identity Management Theory,简称 IMT)、身份协商理论(Identity Negotiation Theory,简称 INT)、文化认同理论(Cultural Identifications Theory)、交际身份认同理论(Communication Theory of

8.1 动态地建构和调适文化身份
Constructing and adjusting cultural identities dynamically

Identity，简称CTI）等。这些理论虽然对身份认同给出了不同的定义，但都或多或少认为，身份认同是和人们对于某一个地区、团体、组织的归属感相关的，涉及个人心理/精神/情感需求这个维度以及社会对个人的要求/需求/期待这个维度。而在文化领域内，个人身份的认同及其调适，实际上是随时随地不断发生的。当一个人来到一个新的文化情境下，可能就需要随时调整自己的文化身份。所以我们说，文化身份认同会在稳定的维持和积极的调整两个维度之间，以具体情境为条件得以动态地建构。如学者顾力行（Steve J. Kulich）建立的 IIMT（Integrated Identity Matrix Theory）身份认同模式（2010），就用三维矩阵（matrix）描摹了个人在自身和外界众多促进或制约因素中动态地调整自己身份认同的过程。

个人身份的确认和调整，和他所处的那个国家的社会结构以及"国家文化"之间是什么关系呢？按照社会功能主义（structural-functionalism）的观点，国家文化是一个包含了社会生活各个方面的系统，其中包括社会结构、人们的行为、价值观和意识形态等，国家文化规定了具体文化现象和个人的行为观念。Holliday 总结了 Weber 的社会行动理论（Social Action Theory）以及 Kumaravadivelu、Fairclough 等学者的文化现实主义（Cultural Realism）和社会建构主义（Social Constructivism）（2010:176；2013:169-170）。这些学者的某些共同理念和社会功能主义并不完全一致，概括而言：一个国家的社会结构并不一定能够完全定义和制约其中具体的文化现象，社会生活的各个方面和社会结构之间是相互对话和影响的关系。因此，对于一个个体的身份认同而言，它具有复杂性，并不是固定的、死板的、一致的，而是碎片化的、个性化的、变化的。具体的文化现象和国家的社会结构之间是对话和互动的关系，个人和社会结构之间也是互动、对话和相互影响的。

It may be hard to imagine that some of the first generation Chinese immigrants who have lived in the United States for nearly 30 years have some discomfort and anxiety when they return to China to visit relatives and friends. One Chinese-American woman said: "Every time I return to China, buying gifts for relatives and friends is quite a headache. If I choose something distinctively American, they will say that you are showing off. If I send them something ordinary, they will laugh at me for I know nothing about the rapid growth of China. They can enjoy a much richer variety of goods than before. Besides, my friends in China tend to care about the economic value of gifts. Such concerns are not common in the United States, where friends prefer unique gifts with special greetings. They don't care much about the economic value of gifts. I feel that when I go back to China, I know neither who I am nor what gifts to bring back."

In fact, this Chinese-American woman is in the midst of "temporary cultural identity confusion". In the process of cultural identification, people often ask "Who I am? Where do I come from? Which group, unit, organization or class do I belong to?" Cultural identity is an important concept that has attracted more and more scholarly attention in the past decades. Although it is often categorized in the discipline of social psychology or sociology, the concept has been more and more explored by applied linguists.

With the development of globalization, various forms of cultural mixing have occurred from time to time. As people's mobility increases, identity changes and anxiety also follow. In different contexts of cultural mixing, people will adopt different models of cultural identification. A more inclusive model includes the following three steps: "integration", which means integrating two or more identities into one, accepting each of them; "alternation", which means using different strategies in different contexts; "synergy", which means that a person, under the influence of different cultures, constructs a new identity that is different from the simple superposition or juxtaposition of several cultures. (Wu, 2016)

The relevant theories of identity/identification currently include Identity Management Theory (IMT), Identity Negotiation Theory (INT), Cultural Identifications Theory, and Communication Theory of Identity (CTI). Although these theories have different definitions of identity, they all hold that identity is more or less related to the sense of belonging to a certain region, group, and organization, and involves the dimension of individual psychological/mental/emotional needs and the dimension of social requirements/needs/expectations for individuals. In the cultural field, the identification and adjustment of personal identity is actually happening anytime and anywhere. When a person comes to a new cultural context, he/she may need to contextually and conditionally adjust his/her cultural identity. Therefore, we say that cultural identity will be dynamically constructed and adjusted on the basis of specific contexts between the two dimensions: stable maintenance and favorable adjustment. For instance, the IIMT (Integrated Identity Matrix Theory) identity model established by Steve J. Kulich (2010) uses a matrix to describe the process by which individuals dynamically adjust their identities despite the stimuli or the constraints from themselves and from the outside world.

What is the relationship between adjustment of personal identity, the social structure of the nation in which he lives, and the "national culture"? According to some theories related to social structural-functionalism, national culture is more or less depicted as a system that encompasses all aspects of social life, including people's behaviors, norms, values, and ideologies. Adrian Holliday has summarized Max Weber's Social Action Theory, and the theories of Cultural Realism and Social Constructivism by such scholars as Kumaravadivelu and Fairclough. (2010: 176; 2013: 169 - 170) Some of the common ideas of these scholars are not quite in line with structural functionalism. These scholars believe that the social structure of a nation does not necessarily completely define and constrain specific cultural phenomena within it; all aspects of social life and human life are in dialogue with the social structure. Therefore, an individual's identification is complex—not fixed, rigid, and consistent, but fragmented, personalized, and changing. The relationship between specific cultural phenomena and a nation-based social structure is a dialogue and interaction. Individuals and a social structure also interact and influence each other.

思考 & 讨论 Reflection and discussion

1. 一个个体在哪些情况下需要调整自己的某个特定身份？

2. 当我们出于平等对话的目的而强调"多样性"（diversity）的时候，我们是不是反而在强调彼此的"不同"？在突出别人和我们"不一样"？要对"别人"区别对待？

3. 一些持有极端想法的建构主义者们甚至认为一切都是在具体情况下随时建构的，没有什么统一、固定的文化现状（cultural reality），你同意吗？

1. Under what circumstances does an individual need to adjust his/her identities?

2. When we emphasize "diversity" for the purpose of equal dialogue, are we also emphasizing "differences"? Are we highlighting our "differences" from others? Are we treating "others" differently?

3. Some constructivists go extreme and believe that everything is constructed on the basis of specific contexts, and there is no unified, fixed cultural reality. Do you agree?

学习者自己的提问和反思 Your own questions and reflections

1. _____

2. _____

3. _____

互动小锦囊 Toolkits for interaction

美国学者米尔斯（2016：131-132）认为，一个认为社会结构是简单清晰的、有规律有条理的、甚至对社会生活各方面具有决定作用的社会学学说是刻板而有局限性的。他在《社会学的想象力》一书中，突出强调了人类生活中生龙活虎的、历史性的、不断处

第八节 动态的文化身份和柔韧的文化疆界
Theme 8　Dynamic cultural identities and pliable cultural boundaries

于时间流动中的各种因素在人们考察和认知社会结构时的作用。他说,社会学的一个最初的、也是持续努力的工作就是将以下两个方面的观点进行结合:

1."有序"的描述:对人类和社会简单的、让人们能够理解的、有规律性的总结和描述;

2."复杂"的描述:能够涵盖人类生活广度和深度的、复杂的总结和描述。

而做到这些,需要我们把社会结构放在曾经发生和正在发生的历史当中去全面对比和理解。

In his book *The Sociological Imagination*, C. Wright Mills (2016:131 - 132) points out the limitations of structural functionalism which tends to provide some simple, orderly, explicit, and even decisive rules of a social structure. He emphasizes the important roles that the verified, vivid, and historical aspects of human lives play in a society. According to him, the first and continuing struggle of social science lies in both an orderly and a disorderly aspect:

1. to come to an orderly understanding of men and the societies requires a set of viewpoints that are simple enough to make understanding possible, yet

2. comprehensive enough to permit us to include in our views the range and depth of the human society.

And to achieve this we need to see a full comparative understanding of the social structures that have appeared and do now exist in world history.

 互动&体验 Interaction

1. 一个个体的文化身份认同过程总离不开自身的心理、精神、情感、认知因素,也离不开环境、和他人关系、原有的文化背景、社会和团体对他的期待等各种因素。你可否试着将这些因素按照一定的逻辑范畴在右图中逐步归纳一下: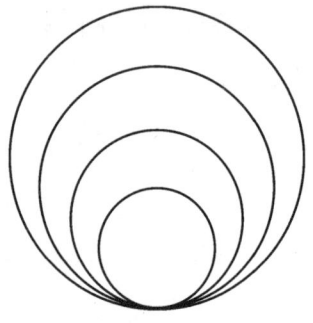

或者(请在下方空白处画出你心中个体文化身份认同与其它各种因素之间的关系示意图):

2. 本节开篇时,提及了一个在回国给亲朋好友送礼时无所适从的美籍华裔女士。你觉得,她的选择困难或身份困惑受到哪些因素的影响?她是否一定需要确定自己的身份归属(到底按照中国人还是按照美国人的方式来买礼物)?如果我们是她,应该如何针对她某个具体朋友的情况做出合适的选择?

3. 20世纪初,四川汶川瓦寺有位土司索季皋,他当时身兼"汶川县团练局长"一职,又是金川江防军总司令部的一个区司令官。他经常阅读报纸杂志,以丰富自己的国内外新知。他也会和喇嘛们以及国民党政府考察民俗或巡视边疆的官员一起讨论时政,以此向来客炫耀。他还请县长帮忙重修土司家谱,认可他是世代忠臣。他这个逐渐学习新知、适应新身份的过程,一方面改变了他作为传统中国边藩土司的本质,另一方面也涓滴改变了传统的华夏边缘。(王明珂,2008)那么,他行为的改变,可能受到哪些个人动机的影响呢?又会受到哪些现实情境、政治语境、文化结构的影响呢?他的行为又怎样调整了原先的文化结构呢?

1. An individual's cultural identification is not only inseparable from his/her own psychological, spiritual, emotional, and cognitive factors, but also inseparable from the environment, his/her relationship with others, the cultural background, the expectations from the society and different groups he/she is involved. Can you try to categorize these factors with certain logics in the following graph?

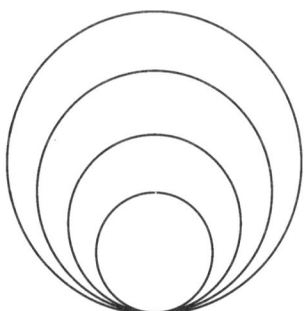

Or you can draw a graph to show the relationship between various factors mentioned and one's identity with your own logical frame below:

2. At the beginning of this section, we talked about a Chinese-American woman who feels confused when she must choose proper gifts for her visit to relatives and friends in China. What factors do you think her dilemma or identity confusion are affected by? Does she really have to determine her own identity (to vote for the "Chinese" or the "American"

way to buy gifts) when buying the gifts? If we were in her place, how should we make the right choices for her different friends?

3. There was a story of a Tibetan chieftain of Wasi Temple in Wenchuan, Sichuan Province named Suo Jigao, in 1930s. Suo Jigao, as a Tibetan, accepted the invitation of commanding Wenchuan County Troops and the Defense Troops for the Guomintang. He often read newspapers and magazines to enrich his knowledge of home and abroad. He would also talk with Tibetan monks in the temple and the Kuomintang officials (sent by the central government to collect folklore or inspect the frontier) about politics, so as to boast to his soldiers and visitors. He also asked the county magistrate to help rebuild the chieftain family tree and recognize his ancestry as generations of loyal officials, following Chinese Han tradition. In this process, on the one hand, he changed his identity as a Tibetan chieftain; on the other hand, he played his small part in blurring and renewing the border of the traditional Chinese Han Territory (Wang, 2008).

What personal motivations might be affecting the changes in his thinking and behavior? Were there other factors, e.g., domestic and world situation, political contexts, and cultural structures? How could his behavior affect the original Tibetan and Chinese Han cultural structures?

8.2 建构柔韧的文化疆界
Constructing pliable cultural boundaries

个人身份的调适,也可以涓滴成一个团体的柔韧边界的形成。在第一节中,我们绘制了一个"云朵状"的文化,并指出:它在具有核心内部的同时,又不断与外界其它文化价值观和行为方式相遇,产生交流,并适时而动态地根据不同的目的进行调整,在边界地带具有开放的、柔韧的、流动互通的特性。因此,这个边界是柔软的;而其韧度,则是来自它内部稳定性向边界方向的延展。这样的疆界,仍然具有保护、认同和统一的作用。

一个文化,总是依托一个群体得以展开。因此,对于一个群体,如族群、国家或一个社会团体来说,其文化特征/文化身份就在内部稳定的维持和边界积极的调整两个维度之间得以动态地建构。在自身权利或利益受到干扰、威胁或动摇时,这个国家/团体会采取不同的身份认同策略来调适,有时是强化固有的文化、宗教、意识形态、语言上的价值坚持,有时则是适度改变,以稳固统治和管理(Starosta,2010)。作为一个个体,需要时时意识到这些语境给自身的身份认知带来的深刻约束和影响。

如果这个团体是一个民族,那么如何积极地维护民族的文化传承,同时又对"异族文化"保持开放的姿态,避免过于极端的民族中心主义(ethnocentrism)和价值观的刻板固守,是我们需要思考的问题。出于身份认同、团体归属感的需要,人们具有一定的民族感情、国家自豪感是必要的,但如果产生下面这些想法或做法,就不利于跨文化交流了:① 把自己所在的群体内习得和接纳的文化习俗和观念当成是天然正确、毋庸置疑的;② 用自己的文化习俗和观念去评判其他的文化习俗和观点,与自己的越相近,我们就越赞同和亲近,反之就越疏远;③(更加极端地认为)自己的文化甚至国家是最正确、最好、最道德、最优秀的;④ 发展出一套否定其它文化理论存在的理论体系。

很多学者在研究身份认同时,还详细探讨了一些重要的概念,如离散(disaporas)、混杂(bybridity)、异质性(heterogeneity)等。部分学者在深入研究种族冲突和身份认同过程中,对"混杂"进行了复杂、深刻的剖析。通常人们认为"混杂"是一种现存的状态

第八节 动态的文化身份和柔韧的文化疆界
Theme 8 Dynamic cultural identities and pliable cultural boundaries

或者是可以作为一种文化身份调适的途径,但一些专家指出这一概念过于理想化、抽象化。比如,Werbner 说,混杂是具有魅力的一个"悖论"(指出它的复杂性和过于理想化特征),它被尊为"强大的阻碍,同时又被视为普通的、普遍的理论"。Mitchell 说 Soja 所谓的"第三空间"(即类似于混杂的一种状态)其实"并不存在,所以它才能完成这些非凡的任务"。(Dirlik,1999:109)

对个人身份认同的讨论还在一直继续下去。有一点可以确定的是,我们的身份往往随着环境、情境的变化而不断得以调整。在跨文化环境里,这个随时的、动态的调整显得尤为重要。经过对一个不熟悉文化形态或观念的探索、倾听、移情,又经过协商和谈判后懂得因地制宜地解决问题,我们是否发现我们有了更强的文化调节能力?并且,我们可以开始反观某一种文化价值观念,是否是世界上唯一正确的文化价值观念?并且是评价其它文化观念和行为的唯一正确标准?我们也可以开始反观我们自己:我们的跨文化能力是否在某种程度上得到了提升?

The adjustment of personal identity can also drip into the formation of the pliable boundary of a group. In 1.1, we draw a "cloud-like" shape of a culture and point out that while it has a "hard" core inside, it constantly meets with other cultural values and behaviors of the outside world, generates communication, and timely and dynamically adjusts itself for different purposes, making the boundary area soft and interactive. In this way, we will see a culture with stable, commonly shared values and norms in the central area and with dynamic interactions in the border areas. The pliability of a culture comes from its internal stability extending towards the dynamic boundary, yet though dynamic, this boundary still functions to protect, identify and unify a group.

A culture is discussed with a social group. Therefore, for a social group, for example, an ethnic group, a country or an organization, its cultural trait/cultural identity is dynamically constructed between the two dimensions of stable internal maintenance and positive adjustment of the boundary. When its rights or interests are disturbed, threatened or shaken, the country/group will adopt different identity strategies to adjust—sometimes to strengthen the existing religious, ideological, linguistic value beliefs, sometimes to make moderate changes in order to consolidate its governance (Starosta, 2010). As an individual, one needs to be aware of the profound constraints and influences these contexts bring to one's own identity.

If this group is a nation, then we need to think about how to actively maintain the cultural heritage of the nation while holding an open attitude towards "alien cultures" so as to avoid extreme ethnocentrism and rigidity in following its own values. It is understandable that out of sense of belonging and identification people tend to feel close to and be proud of their ethnicity or country to some extent. But the following views and behaviors of ethnocentrism are unfavorable to smooth intercultural communication: ① the cultural norms and values that one acquires within his own group are naturally correct and unquestionable. ② use one's own group's norms and values as standards to judge other cultural norms and values, feeling close to those that are similar and feeling distant/repelled/repulsive to those that are "strange" and "different"; ③ one's own cultural norms and values are the most correct, the best, the most moral and the most excellent; ④ develop a whole set of theoretical system to criticize and retort other cultural theories.

In their discussion on identity, some scholars have explored important concepts in detail, e.g. diasporas, hybridity, heterogeneity among others. They conduct a complex and profound analysis of "hybridity" in their in-depth study of ethnic conflicts and identification. Usually, people regard "hybridity" as an existing state or a way to adjust cultural identity, but they point out this concept is too ideal and abstract. For example, Pnina Werbner believes that hybridity is a "paradox", referring to the complexity and over-idealization of it, and it "is celebrated as powerfully interruptive and yet theorized as commonplace and pervasive." Mitchell said what Edward Soja called "the third space" (a state similar to hybridity) "is able to accomplish all these marvelous things, precisely because it does not exist." (Dirlik, 1999: 109)

The discussion on identity can always continue. One thing we may conclude now based on the theories introduced is that one's identity is always under modification and adjustment according to different needs in different environment and contexts. This contextual, dynamic adjustment is very important in intercultural communication. After careful exploring and empathizing with someone in a new cultural phenomenon, and then necessary negotiating and contextual problem-solving, have we experienced more of the intercultural interaction and adjustment? In the meantime, we may start to reflect on our own culture: is it the best and the only correct standard for judging other cultures in the world? We may also start to reflect on ourselves: has our intercultural competence in some way been developed?

思考 & 讨论 Reflection and discussion

1. 多民族国家如美国、加拿大、中国等,是如何协调国家认同和其中每个民族/族群自身的文化认同的?

2. 当有些社会团体或国家为了自身发展而做出开放的姿态时,其结果是导致更多

第八节 动态的文化身份和柔韧的文化疆界
Theme 8 Dynamic cultural identities and pliable cultural boundaries

的分裂还是更多的融合?

3. 你觉得如何去区分民族自豪感和民族中心主义呢?

1. How do multinational countries such as the United States, Canada, and China coordinate the identity of the whole country and the identity of each nationality/ethnic group?

2. When some social groups or countries decide to adopt more open policies for their own development, does that result in more division or more fusion?

3. How do we distinguish national pride, patriotism, and ethnocentrism?

学习者自己的提问和反思 Your own questions and reflections

1. _____
2. _____
3. _____

互动小锦囊 Toolkits for interaction

与民族中心主义相对应的一个概念是民族相对主义(Ethnorelativism)。民族相对主义主张用其它群体的文化理论框架(而不是用自己所在群体的固有文化理论框架)来解释这个群体内人们的文化行为和观念。Ting-Toomey(2007:159)总结 Lukens 和 Bennett 相关理论,用以下图表来描摹交流过程中从民族中心主义到民族相对主义的不同程度:

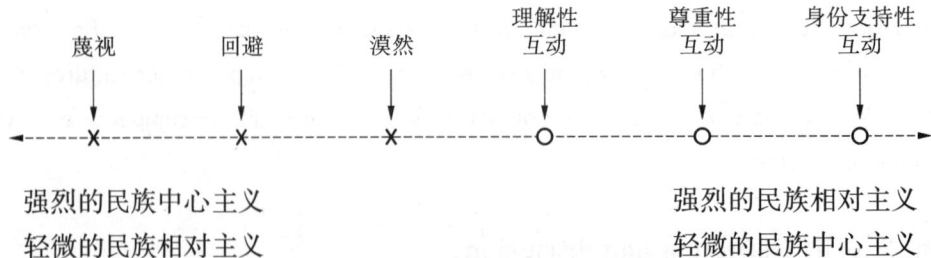

One concept opposite to ethnocentrism is Ethnorelativism. Ting-Toomey (2007: 159) summarizes the related theories of J. Lukens and M. Bennett, and draws the following figure to illustrate the different degrees one can undergo from ethnocentrism to ethnorelativism.

8.2 建构柔韧的文化疆界
Constructing pliable cultural boundaries

According to Ting-Toomey, ethnorelativism "emphasizes the use of out-group members' cultural frame of reference in interpreting their behaviors." (ibid, 158)

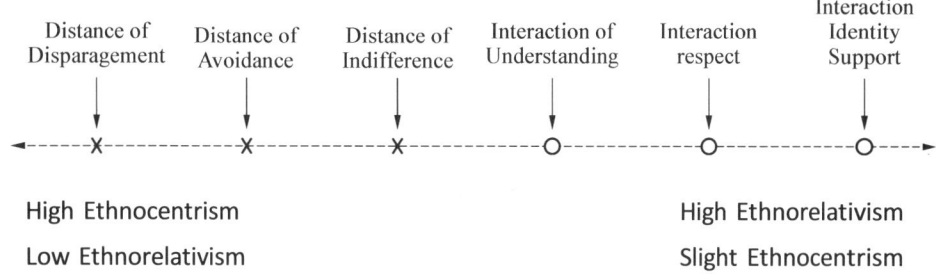

 互动&体验 Interaction

1. 华裔女设计师刘扬在《东西相遇》中曾经用漫画形式表现"东方"和"西方"的差异。比如,在一日三餐、餐具、天气与心情的关系、下属与领导的关系方面,她用下面四幅图表示。

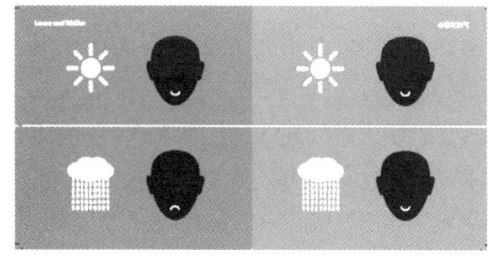

但是我们来看看苏伊是否符合这些描述。苏伊出生在上海,后来去德国留学,现在和德国籍丈夫以及他们的两个孩子定居德国波恩,是德国一家跨国公司的员工,但每个季度她都有30天在上海分公司工作,其它时间在波恩工作。在上海工作期间,她和父母住在她买的一套公寓里。苏伊在这几年中,是如何跨越刘扬漫画中东西方的分割,而协调出自己独特的生活习惯和工作方式的呢?下面是苏伊的自述:

"我这样来回跑已经五年了,表面上看我好像的确是个很分裂很混乱的人,在波恩我中午1点半吃午饭,在上海我中午11点半吃午饭,晚饭呢,如果上班在波恩是晚上八

第八节 动态的文化身份和柔韧的文化疆界
Theme 8 Dynamic cultural identities and pliable cultural boundaries

点半,上海是晚上六点半回家跟父母吃。我累的时候、感冒的时候,还是喜欢喝热茶,我先生慢慢也喜欢喝热茶了,他越来越少喝啤酒了。我在波恩家里时一直是喜欢用微波炉热食物。洗澡时间比较混乱,早上晚上都行,看时间情况。餐具呢,两边我基本上都是随手抓来,筷子、叉子、勺子、盘子还是小碗,不分的。工作中,在上海我比较在意中国内地同事的思维方式和工作作风,对他们注重关系、特别尊重领导这些,我是理解的。在波恩,哈哈,我们有渠道可以投诉甚至罢免领导。好在我们有自己的企业文化,无论是波恩、上海还是其它分公司,很大程度上可以统一来自各个国家员工的行为方式。

对于苏伊,我们可以问出很多问题并加以讨论,比如,苏伊这样的身份协调过程,是真的分裂混乱吗?是稳定的还是不可能长久的?她的行为渐渐发生了哪些变化?可能基于什么原因?以后可能发生什么变化,会基于什么原因发生变化?

2.纪录片《你一定不要错过》展现了过去70年内蒙古电影发展的历程,不少内蒙古电影多次获得电影节重要奖项,也有不少电影用蒙语、由蒙古族演员拍摄,也有一些由蒙汉人员共同组成的摄制团队获得集体大奖。这些在某种程度上反映了汉民族和蒙古族彼此融合、尊重,相互学习来丰润自身的文化。你了解蒙古族历史和文化吗?我们可以找一找这部纪录片,或者类似的纪录片、书籍,来了解一下不同民族的文化也是可以积极地相互接纳和融合的。

3.学者们认为,人们出于不同的原因,会不同程度地、在不同方面具有文化民族主义倾向。可能的原因包括:身份认同的稳定感和安全感、群体团结和稳定、价值观的维持、与外族竞争资源等。不同的方面包括:语言、食物、衣着、建筑、生活方式、环境设计等。不同的程度包括:蔑视、远离、漠不关心、理解、尊重、认同等。

例一:"泱泱大国,不跟娄鼠计较。"
<u>可能给出的分析和评述</u>:出于民族身份认同和稳定感的需求,对其它国家具有蔑视的态度。

例二:"巴黎戴高乐机场里各处的标志牌上怎么只使用英语、法语和中文三种语言呢?"。
<u>可能给出的分析和评述</u>:
(1)法国出于对本国身份的稳定感需求或出于潜在的竞争心态,在语言方面对使

用中文的游客有轻视态度,暗示他们不懂外语,不懂沟通,在机场比其他游客更容易出现问题。

(2) 可能是对中国游客这个庞大的客户群体给予更加尊重和贴心服务。

(3) 也可能仅仅是机场的惯例,给最大流量客户以他们的语言指导。

你还能举出别的例子并进行分析吗?

1. In her book *East Meets West*, the Chinese-American female designer Liu Yang uses comics to depict the differences between the Eastern and the Western Worlds. These concern meals, tableware, the connection between weather and mood, and the relationship between subordinates and leaders. Take the following four pictures as examples.

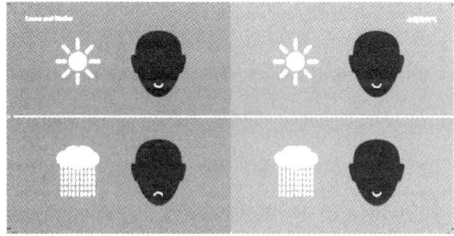

But Suyi's life doesn't seem to fit into these descriptions. Born in Shanghai, Suyi went to Germany to study. Now she lives in Bonn, Germany with her husband and two of her children. She works for a multinational company based in Bonn, but she has to work for 30 days in Shanghai every quarter of the year. While working in Shanghai, she and her parents live in an apartment she bought. In the past few years, how has Suyi crossed the division depicted by Liu Yang's comics and coordinated her unique lifestyle and work pattern? Here is Suyi's self-account:

"I have been shuttling for five years. On the surface I indeed seem to be a very confused person. I have lunch at 1:30 p.m. in Bonn but at 11:30 a.m. in Shanghai. When I work in Bonn, I have dinner at 8:30 p.m. But when I work in Shanghai, I often go home to have dinner with my parents at 6:30 p.m. When I am tired or having a cold,

第八节 动态的文化身份和柔韧的文化疆界
Theme 8　Dynamic cultural identities and pliable cultural boundaries

I'd like to drink hot tea. Gradually, my husband also gets used to hot tea and drinking less and less beer. When I'm at my home in Bonn, I always use the microwave oven to heat up my food. The bath time is quite confusing, for I can do it in the morning or evening, as long as it's convenient. In terms of the tableware, I basically use everything available, chopsticks, forks, spoons, plates or small bowls. When I work in Shanghai, I follow the Chinese colleagues' way of thinking and their work styles, understanding that they pay attention to relationships and respect the leadership. In Bonn,  haha, we have channels to complain about our leaders or even recall them. Fortunately, we have our own corporate culture that can largely unify the behaviors of employees from various countries, whether it is in Bonn, Shanghai or other branches."

Suyi's case raises a lot of questions we can discuss. For example, is her identification really a split and chaotic process? Is it stable or unlikely to last for long? What has changed in her behaviors? What could be the reasons? What changes may occur in the future, and what may be the underlying causes?

2. The documentary *Do Not Miss It* shows the development of the Inner Mongolian film industry over the past 70 years. Many Inner Mongolian films have won important awards at film festivals. There are also films spoken in Mongolian, or played by Inner Mongolian actors. Other films shot by crews of both the Han and the Inner Mongolian nationalities have won collective prizes. To a certain extent, these accomplishments reflect the long integration and established mutual respect between the Han and the Inner Mongolian people, who have learned from each other to enrich themselves. Do you know Inner Mongolian history and culture? We can find this documentary, or similar documentaries and books. Can we explore from multiple perspectives the causes of the integration of the two peoples?

3. Scholars believe that people, for different reasons, have cultural nationalistic tendencies to varying degrees and in different aspects.

——Possible reasons include: a sense of stability and security of identity, group solidarity and stability, maintenance of values, and competition for resources with other groups.

——Different cultural artifacts include: language, food, clothing, architecture, lifestyle, and environmental design.

——Different degrees of cultural nationalism include: contempt, distance, indifference, understanding, respect, and recognition.

Example 1: "A big country will not care about disturbances or attacks from small countries."

Possible analyses and comments:

(1) To highlight the need for national identity and stability. The statement shows contempt for other countries.

(2) Or?

Example 2: English, French and Chinese are the only three languages on the signs at Paris Charles de Gaulle Airport.

Possible analyses and comments:

(1) For the stability of their own identity or due to their potential competitive mentality, they have a disdainful attitude towards Chinese-speaking tourists in terms of language use, suggesting that they understand neither foreign languages nor communication skills and therefore are more likely to have problems at airports than other tourists.

(2) The French people want to show greater respect and provide warmer service to the huge customer group of Chinese tourists.

(3) It is just the regulation from the airport that they indicate places with the languages according to the passage flows.

Can you think of other examples and try to analyze them?

第八节 动态的文化身份和柔韧的文化疆界
Theme 8 Dynamic cultural identities and pliable cultural boundaries

援引阅读 Quoted readings

"最后,以建构主义思维方式定义的文化不包含文化绝对性,即没有普遍通用的文化比较标准。我们比较文化的任何标准都是为那个目的而建构的。因此,作为观察者的我们应该清楚那些标准的适当性。……建构主义并不排除对文化作出判断。实际上,用建构主义比用相对论的思维方式更容易判断。在纯粹的文化相对论看来,不存在任何普遍标准,也没有创造此标准的机制。而在建构主义中,虽然还是没有普遍标准,但有这样的机制,即创建类别或范畴,它可以建构可供人类普遍应用的评价标准。观察者的技能就是为了达到理解文化差异的目的而建构中性标准,然后运用判断标准对行为进行判断。"(第38-39页)

——米尔顿·J·贝内特编著.关世杰、何悝译.《跨文化交流的建构与实践》.北京:北京大学出版社,2012年.

"由于现代化的激励,全球政治正沿着文化的界线重构。文化相似的民族和国家走到一起,文化不同的民族和国家则分道扬镳,以意识形态和超级大国关系确定的结盟让位于以文化和文明确定的结盟,重新划分的政治界线越来越与种族、宗教、文明等文化的界线趋于一致,文化共同体正在取代冷战阵营,文明间的断层线正在成为全球政治冲突的中心界线。"(第105页)

——塞缪尔·亨廷顿著.周琪等译.《文明的冲突》.北京:新华出版社,2012年.

"外国的文化民族主义大致起自德国的浪漫派哲学家和批评家赫尔德(J. G. von Herder, 1744-1803)。当时的西方,英国和法国的发展均先进于德国,在德国的民族心理中,便生出一种不敢正视也不愿承认的自卑感。他们出于自尊,进而求精神上的'自我安慰'、'自我保护',于是以赫尔德为代表的知识分子便批判对英法的现代化事业贡献极大的启蒙理性,大讲本国日耳曼文化的'民族特性'、'国民精神',强调文化相对主义,否认各民族文化之间的相通、共同之处,反对文化的普世性。马克思曾批评这种民族主义是'头足倒置'——只敢在头脑中完成邻国在政治上已经完成的变革。……现在提倡构建'和谐社会'、'和谐文化'。'和谐'(harmony)与'单一'、'一律'正相反,而是多样性、不同性相融合、相济的结果。显然,封闭、保守、排他的文化民族主义对建设'和谐社会'的文化是极为不利的。"(第5-6页)

——董健《全球化与文化民族主义》.何成洲主编.《跨学科视野下的文化身份认同》.北京:北京大学出版社,2011年.

"How can we suppose that whatever is accidental excludes the rational when at the origin of every habit is a caprice, and at the base of every natural law, in the words of John

Stuart Mill, an 'arbitrary classification of causes'? The air, like the sea, is furrowed with invisible routes followed by birds and boats in their periodic migrations. Because they are so unvarying despite their meanderings, many of these paths have a semblance of necessity, of law based on nature... The sociologists of certain schools should think of this when they make their science into a seeking and formulating of supposed laws of evolution which subject the social transformations of all peoples, regardless of their reciprocal borrowings, to the same itinerary decided, to some extent, in advance."(pp.93 – 94)

——Tarde, G. (2016). *Communication and Social Influence*. Beijing: Chinese Communication University Press.

"Apparently transparent, hybridity is in actuality quite an elusive concept that does not illuminate but rather renders invisible the situations to which it is applied—not by concealing them, but by blurring distinctions among widely different situations. Pnina Werbner has observed as a 'paradox' of the fascination with hybridity that it 'is celebrated as powerfully interruptive and yet theorized as commonplace and pervasive.' If hybridity is indeed pervasive, it is in and of itself meaningless—if everything is hybrid, then there is no need for a special category of hybrid—and can derive meaning only from the concrete historical and structural locations that produce it."(p.108)

——Dirlik, A. (1999). Bringing history back in: Of diasporas, hybridities, places, and histories. *Review of Education, Pedagogy, and Cultural Studies*, 21:2, 95 – 131.

第九节
反思和衡量你的跨文化能力

Theme 9
Reflections and assessments on your IC

第九节 反思和衡量你的跨文化能力
Theme 9 Reflections and assessments on your IC

9.1 跨文化能力测试必要性和标准的讨论
IC assessment: difficult yet necessary

反思自己"跨文化经历"中的心态和言行,可以在它之前、中间或之后随时进行。只要有跨文化意识,这种反思就存在。反思的内容可以包括:我今天有没有随意生气、发脾气、对人有不善、不耐烦甚至恶意攻击的言行?我这样说这样想是不是一种"跨文化的方式"?我怎样才能更好地保有自己,同时又愉快地与人交往?我的跨文化策略是不是采取得比较得当?我的跨文化能力有没有得到提升?

在过去二十年里,在不同的学科领域,人们不断尝试,并提供了几十种与跨文化能力相关的测量标准、方法和工具。这些方法和工具帮助人们通过不同的方式反思自己应对和管理跨文化交流的技巧策略,同时它们本身也在经受反思和质疑,经常受到各种批评,比如:缺乏统一客观的标准、不够稳定、测量因素不够全面、干扰因素太多、成本过高等。我们在序言和第一节里就提到,与跨文化能力相关的概念名称、模式、构成因素等纷繁复杂,如果连基本的名称及其内涵界定都确定不了,如何确定其评价标准?更谈不上开发测量方法和工具了。

持激烈立场的学者甚至质疑,跨文化能力是不是根本就不可以去测量?比如 Borghetti(2017)就质疑跨文化测量的可行性。她发现在跨文化能力测试过程中,测试者出于各种目的,产生对被测者不公平和不公正的现象。此外,人们的一些性格本身值得尊重,不应该一味地提倡甚至要求人们去突破和改变自己的个性,比如有些人性格害羞内向,不愿意过多地交流,有些人性格直爽果断,不喜欢慢慢地去判断。因此,跨文化测试其实是没有必要也无法做到的。

中国人说"做事要有分寸,要把握好'度'",这个实在是精妙。我们发现,关于文化的继承还是开放、每个人价值观的坚守还是突破、在跨文化能力中对每个人价值观和性格的尊重还是突破提升、偏向文化相对稳定的结构还是更多地选择其建设功能等,都涉及一个"度"字。同一个人在不同的时间、地点、情境下,出于不同的动机和目的,也往往采取不同的策略。因此,所谓"因地制宜"四个字,可能只能意会,不能言传吧。

但无论如何,总体来说,如果我们认同现实中国际化形势日趋纷繁复杂,多元文化环

9.1 跨文化能力测试必要性和标准的讨论
IC assessment: difficult yet necessary

境日益增多,那我们就应该认同跨文化交流和对话的必要性,就应该去提倡和鼓励提升人们的跨文化能力。而既然认同跨文化能力是需要提升、可以提升的,那么我们也就应该认可跨文化能力需要去反思、衡量和评估,并研究其可行性。至于是否像自然科学那样可以做到准确的测量,我们认为是不可能的。那到底怎样才可能做出一个基本科学的衡量呢?

Reflection on our attitudes and behaviors through the intercultural tunnel can be done before, during and after the process. This kind of reflection goes along with our awareness of "passing through the tunnel". We can ask questions like: Am I being intercultural by thinking, saying or doing in this way? How can I stick to my own cultural values while interacting pleasantly with others? Is the strategy I am taking adequate or not? Have I improved my intercultural competence after relatively passing through this tunnel?

For the past two decades, people in different fields have been exploring and have developed scores of standards, methods and tools for evaluating and assessing Intercultural Competence (IC). These methods and tools help people to reflect and improve their skills used in IC, but in the meantime these methods and tools have also been undergoing reflection, criticism, and assessment. They are often questioned for incoherent standards, unstable supervision, incomplete elements, too many interfering factors, or high costs. We have earlier mentioned that the related conceptions, connotations, modes and components are too overlapping and interwoven to make clear and stable standards for any possible IC assessment, let alone the development of tools and methods.

Some scholars even go as far as questioning whether it is possible to assess IC at all. Claudia Borghetti (2017) challenges the feasibility of IC assessment partly by challenging the fairness and power equality during the assessment procedure. Also, how should we take into consideration the roles people's personalities play in intercultural communication? Should we take introversion and shyness into measuring "openness"? Should we fully respect people who are introverted and shy without insisting their "breaking through" their characters? Should we respect people who are resolute and quick enough to make decisions by not judging them as "not delaying judgment"? Therefore maybe intercultural competence cannot be evaluated after all indeed.

Chinese ancestors always told us to "do deeds with appropriateness and adequate 'degree'". This is so true. We can find a necessity of "adequate degree" between everything: between adhering to one's own culture and opening to other cultures; between respecting people's personality and gearing it in a direction that will bring about a more pleasant communication; between keeping the stable dimension of a culture and extending the dynamic dimension of a culture... Furthermore, an individual may take up strategies out of different motives and purposes with the change of the place, time, and context. The Chinese idiom "take adequate actions contextually" may exactly address this complicated situation but may only be understood if we are able to read beyond the words.

Generally speaking, if we acknowledge the growing globalization and mobilization in today's world, which leads to a more diversified cultural environment, we will see the necessity of intercultural dialogues, thus we need to identify the skills needed for fruitful or effective intercultural dialogues. If we see skills as important and necessary in intercultural dialogues, we see the necessity to develop, reflect on and assess those skills. We then need to work on how to make the assessments feasible and operable. Yet, we think it is impossible and the wrong direction to construct assessment modes or tools as accurate and as digital-based as those in natural science research. Then, how should we come as closely as possible to some scientific assessments of intercultural competence?

思考 & 讨论 Reflection and discussion

1. 文化价值观念以及人们的日常交流心态，是可以用数据测量的吗？

2. 我们有的时候选择沉默，不愿意多交流，是跨文化能力强还是弱的表现？可以举例说明。

3. "对话"的内涵有哪些？人们进行对话的目的和意图有哪些呢？

1. Can we calculate cultural values and people's attitudes during intercultural communication in a mathematical way?

2. Sometimes we choose to keep silent or walk away without any willingness to communicate. Can this be judged as acquiring a strong or a weak ability in intercultural communication?

3. What is a dialogue? Why do people hold dialogues?

学习者自己的提问和反思 Your own questions and reflections

1. _____

2. _____

3. _____

互动小锦囊 Toolkits for interaction

根据 Geertz(1973:20-21)的看法，对人类社会生活面貌的总体描述是一种人类学上的、质性的研究,而不是一种量化的实证性研究。它可以通过"ethnography"(在跨文化研究领域可翻译为"文化生活志")这样一种进行实地调查并诠释各种文化符号的研究方法得以"捕捉"和"描绘"(也就是说,经过某种解释和再加工),来重新展现人们的文化生活面貌,这种方式至少具有以下四个特征:

(1) 它是"诠释性"的;

(2) 它的"诠释性"所对应的是社会性话语的流动性;

(3) 这个"诠释"过程是试图将这样的社会性话语从"已经被说完"后正在消失的时刻拯救出来,然后把它固定在"可以被看到"的方式中;

(4) 这种"诠释"是以小见大的(即在对细微状态的诠释中揭示宏达的文化或社会行为特征)。

According to Clifford Geertz (1973:20 – 21), a general, overall description of social actions is more of a qualitative interpretation than conclusions drawn from empirical statistics. This kind of description can be drawn with "ethnography", an intellectual effort both in research paradigms and in methodology in social anthropological research. He concludes at least four characteristics of ethnographic description:

(1) It is interpretive;

(2) What it is interpretive of is the flow of social discourse;

(3) The interpreting involved consists of trying to rescue the "said" of such discourse from its perishing occasions and fix it in perusable terms;

(4) It is microscopic (by realizing that social actions are comments on more than themselves; that where an interpretation comes from does not determine where it can be impelled to go.)

 互动&体验 Interaction

1. 年轻的你,正在工作的你,退休了的你,喜欢旅行吗?你能找到关于旅行的意义是什么?我们来写几条(即使你不喜欢旅行,它仍然是有意义的,不是吗?):

★ _____
★ _____
★ _____
★ _____

第九节 反思和衡量你的跨文化能力
Theme 9　Reflections and assessments on your IC

2. 关于我们的生活，我们都在不经意间通过各种方式进行了记录，比如日记、博文、朋友圈、个人公众号、家庭相册等。我们找个时间，翻看一下过去的这些生活点滴，回忆下和别人进行交流的各种瞬间，当时发生了什么？你当时的感觉是怎样的？你现在再回忆起来，心情又是怎样的？

3. 在下面这些话题里面，选取一些你比较熟悉的（或者另外找一些你自己熟悉的话题），然后聊一聊，你是通过怎样的一些途径，经过不断地观察、体会、理解，一步一步慢慢了解它们的？更为重要的是，是什么撬动了你并逐步改变了你的看法呢？

```
量子力学          每天走路一万步          中国雾霾          西药
在中国当一名大学老师        养一只猫咪            意大利面
日本茶道        我的好朋友××          英国女王伊丽莎白
阿根廷          大英博物馆中国展厅          食品安全
弗莱明戈        其他话题……
```

选一个话题，对这个话题，你第一次初步理解的含义是：
理解途径：
书籍　电影　与陌生人聊天　朋友圈　微博　亲戚或朋友聊天　网络　课堂　报纸杂志　演讲会

第二次深入了解后你的理解变成了：
理解途径：
书籍　电影　与陌生人聊天　朋友圈　微博　亲戚或朋友聊天　网络　课堂　报纸杂志　演讲会

第三次深入了解后你的理解又变成了：
理解途径：
书籍　电影与陌生　人聊天　朋友圈　微博　亲戚或朋友聊天　网络　课堂　报纸杂志　演讲会

第四次深入了解后你的理解又变成了：
理解途径：

书籍　电影　与陌生人聊天　朋友圈　微博　亲戚或朋友聊天　网络　课堂　报纸杂志　演讲会

……
……

是哪些因素撬动了你原先的理解呢？

1. Are you young, still studying and working or have you retired? Do you like travelling? No matter if you like it or not, travelling has its own significances. Shall we list them below?

★ _____
★ _____
★ _____
★ _____

2. We document our daily lives through all kinds of means, no matter if you realize this or not. For example, we write diaries and blogs, we twitter, we write WeChat posts, and we make family photo albums. We can find a time to sit down and look again at these momentary glimpses in our lives, when we can have dialogues with ourselves, with our family and friends, and with this world. What happened then? How did you feel? How are you feeling now when recalling those moments?

第九节 反思和衡量你的跨文化能力
Theme 9 Reflections and assessments on your IC

3. There are some topics in the block that you might get to understand during a gradual process. Which ones are you familiar with? (You may find other topics you are familiar with that are not listed below). Can you tell us through which channels and by which steps you have come to understand these topics so far? Maybe more importantly, what situation triggered the change of your understanding of them?

> quantum theory   hiking for 10 km every week   haze in China
> Chinese medicine   working as a university teacher   raising
> a cat at home   spaghetti   Japanese Teaism   my friend
> who...   Queen Elizabeth   Argentina   Chinese Hall in
> British Museum   food safety   Flamingo   other topics...

Choose a topic. As to this topic, your understanding of it for the first time you encountered it was:

Your means of understanding it were (you may tick them off or circle them out):
Books   movies   chatting with strangers   WhatsApp/Facebook   chatting with family and friends   Internet   newspapers and magazines   lectures   classes
---
As to this topic, your understanding of it for the second time you encountered it was:

Your means of understanding it were (you may tick them off or circle them out):
Books   movies   chatting with strangers   WhatsApp/Facebook   chatting with family and friends   Internet   newspapers and magazines   lectures   classes
---
As to this topic, your understanding of it for the third time you encountered it was:

Your means of understanding it were (you may tick them off or circle them out):
Books   movies   chatting with strangers   WhatsApp/Facebook   chatting with family and friends   Internet   newspapers and magazines   lectures   classes
---
As to this topic, your understanding of it for the fourth time you encountered it was:

9.1 跨文化能力测试必要性和标准的讨论
IC assessment: difficult yet necessary

Your means of understanding it were (you may tick them off or circle them out):

Books   movies   chatting with strangers   WhatsApp/Facebook   chatting with family and friends   Internet   newspapers and magazines   lectures   classes

What are the elements that triggered the change of your understanding each time?

第九节 反思和衡量你的跨文化能力
Theme 9 Reflections and assessments on your IC

9.2 结合多种手段来衡量跨文化能力
Assessing IC with combination of different methods

在过去二十年左右的时间里,国外学者们不断研究跨文化能力评估的可行性,并提出和尝试一些测量标准、模式、方法和工具,如 VOS、CCAL、TIP、ICIS、INCA、IDA、AIE 等(Spencer-Oatey & Franklin,2010:173-198;Deardorff,2006)。中国学者也在不断开发和创建适合中国人的跨文化能力测评体系和模式。(如杨述伊,2013;甘小亚等,2018)

就目的来看,这些测量模式和工具有的是出于教学目的,有的出于研究目的,有的是出于个人学历进修的需要,有的则是企业管理的需要,有的是针对个体能力发展做出评估,有的是针对整个团体应对陌生文化的能力做出评估;这些方法和工具的形式和内容也不一而足,有调查表、有访谈、日记、选择题答卷、表演记录、迷你剧,或兼而有之;就评估角度来看,有的是以自我测评为主,有的是他人评价为主,有的是自评与他评结合,包括综合专家、访问者、被访问者、同伴、第三方观察者等多种角度的意见。

目前的趋势来看,人们更多地赞成和选择角度多样化、长期跟踪与短期描述结合、细微观察和宏观反思结合、主观与客观结合的测量方法,来代替单一、片面、刻板、短期的测量方法。在这里,我们简单介绍下第一部分中提到的 ethnography("文化生活志")这个方法,不少跨文化能力测试方法都以此为基础展开。

Ethnography 是人类学研究中的一个概念,Geertz(1973)曾专门详细讨论这个概念。这个概念跟对文化的定义、文化的研究方法息息相关。Geertz 认为,文化是活生生的、多面的、流动的,文化的表现形式不但是"纷繁复杂"和"交织一处"(10)的,尤为重要的是,文化是社会生活的"象征性行为"(10),而不是某种"固定的模式和思维框架"(10),所以,对文化的理解应该是"诠释性"(20)的。他所理解的社会人类学中"文化生活志"这一方法突破了课本中把它当作具体科研方法的定义(如建立友好关系、寻找合适的采访对象、将口述内容转化为文字内容、建立家谱或族谱、给访问区域绘制地图、撰写地方志等行为),而成为一种具有"诠释性"过程的思维方式和研究方法。在他看来,以"文化生活志"方法揭示某种文化的内涵和特性是一种"符号学意义上的"(5)、"思维方式上的努力"(6)。

不少学者和跨文化能力教育者、评估者赞同这个观点,并尝试把这个方法用于整个或部分的跨文化能力评估模式和过程中,采用日志、采访、记录和转码、解释等方式来对某一个个体的跨文化能力进行综合评价,比如"文件夹"(Portfolio)模式及随后发展起来的"跨文化经历自传"(AIE)两种评估方式,都具有"搜集"、"记录"、"整理"跨文化学习者一段时期内的各种感受和表现,从而"诠释"、"衡量"和"总结"他的跨文化发展水平的特征。

根据 Deardorff(2006:250 - 251)组织的一项调查,"跨文化学者们认为最佳的跨文化能力评估途径是综合质性和量性的各种方法"。无论哪种评估方式在哪种情况下具有哪种程度的可行性,我们都应该认同,在"跨文化通道"的整个过程中人们需要经常性回顾和总结,来不断感受自身跨文化能力的动态变化,从而调整"僵硬"和"别扭"之处,并预见今后发展的方向。评估本身,就是跨文化能力的一个组成部分,最终参与某种文化整体上的变迁和调整。

在即将结束所有介绍和活动之前,我们想最终描绘我们心目中的文化:文化在相对一段时间内是稳定的,但最终是不断生成和流动的。它先是通过生动活泼、细碎点滴的日常而转化为某种可读的但永远词不达意的表述,然而它又因为不受社会结构的规束,而会在某些具体的情境中此起彼伏地展现出短暂的新景象,并最终在漫长岁月里汇聚成一个相对崭新的总体历史面貌。它就这样生生不息,承载起人类所有关于物质和精神的生活及其记忆。而我们的每一次微小短暂的跨文化对话,都是构成一幅更美的历史图景的切实努力。

For the past two decades people from different research fields have explored and proposed some IC assessment standards, modes, tools and methods, such as VOS, CCAL, TIP, ICIS, INCA, IDA, AIE (Spencer-Oatey & Franklin, 2010: 173 - 198; Deardorff, 2006), including Chinese scholars who endeavor to develop IC assessment system and models that are more suitable for Chinese (e.g., Yang, 2013; Gan et al. 2018). The purposes of some of these systems and models are for IC teaching, some for research, some for personal advancement, and some for enterprise management. The forms and contents of these assessments vary, too. It can be either: questionnaires, interviews, diaries, multiple-choice test papers, documentation of performances, mini-dramas, roleplays, or a combination of some of these. The perspectives of assessments range from self-reflection and assessment, peer review and evaluation to evaluation from the expert, the interviewer, or from any third party.

Now more and more researchers tend to use synchronized methods to do IC assessment, which combine short-term observation with long-term observation, macro description with micro description, and subjective evaluation with objective evaluation... so as to replace the simplified, arbitrary, stereotyped, and momentary way of judging. Here we give a brief introduction to "ethnography", the term we mentioned in 9.1., on the basis of

which many IC assessment methods are developing.

Ethnography is a conception in anthropology that Clifford Geertz (1973) discusses in particular when he tries to reveal the essence of culture. According to Geertz, human behavior is seen as "symbolic action"(10). On the surface data collected about human behaviors look "superimposed upon" and "knotted into" each other (10), because culture is itself vivid, fluid, and dynamic. Therefore a certain culture is something "interpretive"(20) rather than "a patterned conduct" or "a frame of mind"(10). His discussion of ethnography from socio-anthropological perspective breaks through its original function of a mere research method (establishing rapport, selecting informants, transcribing texts, taking genealogies, mapping fields, keeping a diary), and sees it as "an intellectual effort" that is "made towards grasping what anthropological analysis amounts to as a form of knowledge" (6) in a "semiotic" way (5).

Darla K. Deardorff (2006: 250 – 251) reports in her study that "according to the intercultural scholars, the best way to assess intercultural competence is through a mix of qualitative and quantitative measures." Indeed quite some IC educators and assessors design diaries, interviews, documentation, transcripts, and interpretation into IC assessment models or methods on the basis of ethnography. Take "portfolio" and "Autobiography of Intercultural Encounters"(AIE) as examples. Both of these two assessment methods include collecting, recording, sorting out, coding and decoding people's feeling and behaviors when passing through an intercultural tunnel, to finally interpret, evaluate and draw conclusions about, to some degree, their intercultural competence.

Whichever means we take, whatever situation we see the feasibility, and to whatever extent we can do in IC assessment, we need a consensus that people need to often reflect on their attitudes and behaviors when passing through an intercultural tunnel, and try to experience all the dynamic changes happening along the whole process. Hopefully in doing this they can step out of the "stiff" and "awkward" corners in their lives and see how they could possibly do under similar context in the future in a more creative way. The assessment itself, is in the end part of intercultural competence and participates in the whole process of cultural exchange and adjustment.

Before we close all the discussions and interactions in this book, we would like to repeat that a culture, though in the necessity of beholding stable values, norms and traditions for a certain period of time, is forever vivid and flowing. It is in the first place described by some language interpretive yet with "differánce" on the basis of decoding daily human behaviors, and then is interfered and challenged by some "new" phenomena popping up here and there in specific contexts. Through a long period it will then take a relatively new look on the whole basis. A culture is growing like this endlessly, storing and bearing all physical and spiritual lives and their memories in human history. While making every small effort in our intercultural dialogue, we will contribute a step to the betterment of culture and human civilization.

思考 & 讨论 Reflection and discussion

1. 用单项或多项选择题的方法对人们的跨文化能力进行测试,可能会有哪些弊端?

2. 你认为语言和文字能够完完全全地表述事物本身的面貌吗?为什么?

3. 人们都知道文化的内涵是变化的,人们对文化内容的认知是变化的,但人们有时又非常坚持自己的原则和传统。那么变化到底在哪些情况下才会发生呢?

1. What could possibly be the disadvantages of providing single- or multiple-choice test papers to do IC assessment?

2. Do you think languages and texts can faithfully reveal an event? Why?

3. Many people have learned that cultural values and norms are undergoing changes and people's cognitions of certain cultures are undergoing changes, too. But on many occasions people simply stick to their cultural values and norms in a non-negotiable way. Then, what could be the conditions and elements that may trigger any change in our well-guarded values?

学习者自己的提问和反思 Your own questions and reflections

1. _____
   _____
2. _____
   _____
3. _____
   _____

第九节 反思和衡量你的跨文化能力
Theme 9 Reflections and assessments on your IC

互动小锦囊 Toolkits for interaction

Autobiography of Intercultural Encounters(AIE),"跨文化经历反思问答卷"(Byram et al,2009),是欧洲委员会在语言学习和教育方面提倡的一种评估方法,其中重要的组成内容就是鼓励对语言学习中跨文化能力的学习和评估。这份学习材料除了给出各种相关概念的详细注释外,专家们还给出了一份简短的理论讨论清单。这份清单建议在讨论语言问题时需要考虑以下方面的内容,我们可以从其中看出跨文化能力学者们深厚的人文关怀和深刻的社会思考,从而看出点滴的跨文化努力与人类活动、国家与社会发展、历史进程之间密不可分的联系。

(a) 文化
(b) 多元文化的社会
(c) 对待其它文化的态度
(d) 公民身份和国籍
(e) 历史和文化、他者、公民身份
(f) 多重身份:对自我如何诠释
(g) 认识其它的文化:对他人如何诠释
(h) 欧洲语境中多元性的功能:多语言主义
(i) 欧洲语境中多元性的功能:多语言性和跨文化性
(j) 积极的公民身份和跨文化公民身份

Autobiography of Intercultural Encounters (AIE) (Byram et al, 2009) is an assessment model developed for language teaching and education by the Council of Europe. One initiative of developing it is to encourage learning and assessing intercultural competence in language learning. Besides exploring into related conceptions and theories, the designers also give a list of discussion in certain aspects related to those conceptions and theories, from which not only can we see the deep concern of human well-beings and societies from the intercultural scholars, but also the deep, close connection between tiny efforts in intercultural communication and grand social development in the long human historical progress.

(a) culture;
(b) multicultural societies;
(c) attitudes to other cultures;
(d) citizenship and nationality;
(e) history and culture, other, citizenship;

(f) multi-identities: interpreting the self;
(g) perception of people from other cultures: interpreting the other;
(h) Functioning in the European context of plurality: plurilingualism;
(i) Functioning in the European context of plurality: pluriculturality and interculturality;
(j) Active citizenship and intercultural citizenship

 互动&体验 Interaction

1. 泉州是中国一个非常著名的多文化旅游地。请大家在网络上搜索一些讲述泉州历史和文化的资料。如果有条件,可以自己去泉州旅行,看一看当地的建筑,品一品当地的小吃。如果你愿意,你还可以读一读《泉州讲古新编》这本书。这本书兼有地方志和地方风俗演绎两种文类,在掺杂闽南话的奇特故事讲述中,你既可以读到像历史经验的记录,又可以领略历史风情的展演。(吴建生主编,2008):

在了解泉州文化的过程中,我们可以独自思考或者和伙伴们讨论一下下面这些问题:
- 你感受到泉州哪些多元文化的因素?
- 哪些是你觉得新鲜的、喜欢的?为什么?
- 哪些是你觉得不适应、不喜欢的?为什么?

对于泉州文化中你不适应、不喜欢的,在经过前面几个章节的跨文化技巧互动后,
- 有没有试着放松你的心态,延迟你的判断,多去了解相关的知识?
- 你在态度或语言、行为上有没有变化?如果有,你是怎样调整的?如果没有,为什么?

2. 中国人对于外国人见面和再见时"拥抱"这样一个风俗,觉得很平常,电影和生活中见过很多。但我们看看梅佳怎么说。梅佳出生在中国,九十年代初她25岁时嫁给了一个比利时人,并随他迁往比利时南部一个小镇定居,至今已经在那里生活了近二十年。说起"拥抱",她仍然津津乐道:一开始我就以为外国人打招呼嘛,就相互抱一抱。这个谁不知道啊。后来我才慢慢发现这个动作其实非常复杂,含义颇深,比如我先生:

——跟他的好友安妮,只是相互用一只胳膊简单抱一抱,脸颊只贴一面而已。

第九节 反思和衡量你的跨文化能力
Theme 9 Reflections and assessments on your IC

——跟安妮的丈夫乔尼，关系非常好，但他们俩从来不互相拥抱，只是握手。

——跟他关系一般的一个女同事罗娜，每次见面和再见都要一边拥抱，一边来回贴面三次。

——跟他的弟弟，每次见面和再见都是握手。

——跟他爸爸，有时握手，有时拥抱。

——跟他的儿子，每次见面和再见都拥抱一次，但是不贴面。

——跟我回中国时，见到我的闺蜜小欣，虽然他们语言不通，平时也没有来往，但每次他们见面都要拥抱并贴面一次。

梅佳说，她花了好几年时间，来观察比利时人"拥抱"这个事情，每次她都有"搞不懂"、"又不懂了"、甚至"一惊一乍"的感觉。她不停地观察并不断问她先生，慢慢才真正理解"拥抱"这个风俗到底对每个比利时人意味着什么，他们又是怎样通过"拥抱"这个举止来展现社会关系和社交状态的。大家说说看，梅佳的先生跟他家人或朋友不同的拥抱方式，可能说明了他和他们之间关系的哪些情况？

3. 你愿意回想一次让你非常愉快或非常不愉快、但至今记忆犹新的跨文化经历吗？我们来试着一起描述和记录当时的细节，并通过这种方式来体会和评估我们的跨文化能力，促使我们今后再次进入"跨文化通道"时能够表现得更加自如、轻松、灵活和有创造力。请试着把下面的内容做进一步补充：

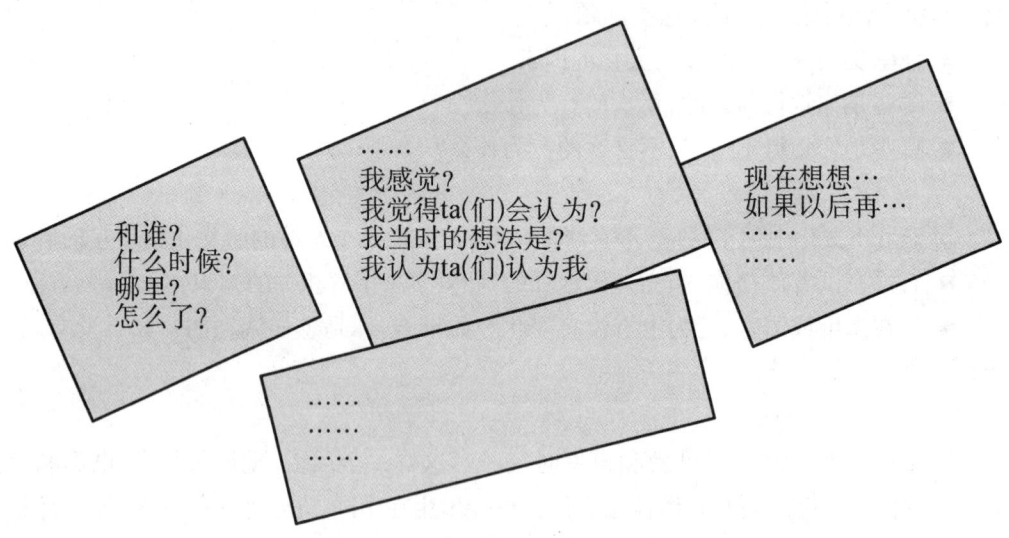

1. Please read the following text.

Quanzhou is a seaport city in Fujian Province, China. In its long history, the city has been greatly influenced by other cultures through overseas business with other countries. In the city, Buddhist temples, Taoist "Guan"s, the worship houses of the local sea gods and land gods, the churches as well as Mosques, locate side by side. The local cuisine of Quanzhou also has complex origins from other places. Please search for more information about the history and cultures in Quanzhou. If you had a chance, you may go and visit the city.

■ After further exploration of the history and cultures in Quanzhou, do you find it a multi-cultural city?

■ Which cultural elements make you feel fresh, new and somewhat like it? Why?

■ Which cultural elements make you feel uneasy, unpleasant and disgusted? Why?

■ After discussing some skills in passing through "intercultural tunnel", have you tried to relax yourself and delay your judgment? Have you tried to learn more background information about any troubling elements?

■ Have you changed your judgment somehow after learning more background information? If yes, how? If not, why?

2. Hugging is not an unfamiliar western cultural tradition in many Chinese eyes. We have seen it in movies or experienced in reality when travelling to some countries. But let us read a bit how Meijia experienced this tradition in Belgium.

Meijia was born in China and in the early 90s of last century she married to a Belgian young man, and when she was 25 years old they moved to live in Belgium. She has now been living in a small town in southern Belgium for almost 20 years. Each time when talking about the "hugs", she has a lot to say.

At the very beginning, I thought it very common and easy. It is all about people greeting each other when they meet and when they bid goodbye. Yet later on I found this posture really bears complicated meanings. I see my husband:

—with his close friend Ann, he just hugs her with one arm and just one kiss in the air on one cheek;

—with his very close friend, Frank, Ann's husband, he never hugs him, but only shakes one hand;

—with his female colleague Rona, they always hug each other and kiss in the air on both cheeks for three times when they meet and when they say goodbye;

—with his younger brother, they always shake hand, without any hugs or kisses;

—with his dad, he sometimes shakes hands with him and sometimes hugs him;

—with his son, they always hug, but never kiss each other;

—with my best girlfriend in China, whom he seldom sees and cannot communicate in any language, they would hug and kiss in the air on the cheeks once.

Meijia said she spent quite some years understanding this "simple" gesture, which confused her again and again, and even shocked her. By asking her husband and keeping observations, she gradually came to realize how Belgians socialize with hugs and kisses contextually. What kind of relationship would you describe respectively between Meijia's husband and each person around him?

3. Are you willing to recall some very impressive experiences through an "intercultural tunnel"? Let's try to describe one encounter and note down some details then, and try to reflect or evaluate our intercultural competence. Hopefully in this way we will know how to adjust our thinking and behaviors in the future to be more at ease, relaxed, flexible and creative. Now try to ask the questions or complete the sentences in the blocks.

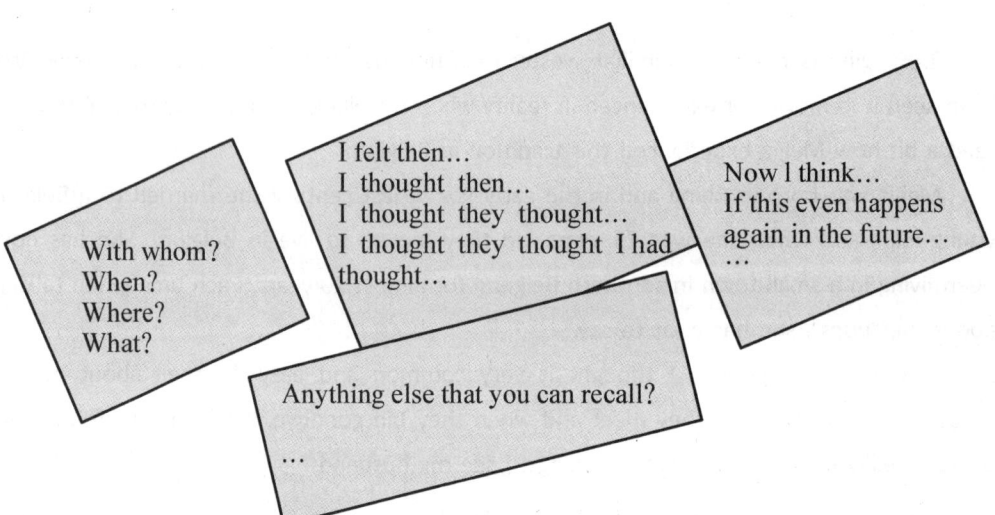

9.2 结合多种手段来衡量跨文化能力
Assessing IC with combination of different methods

援引阅读 Quoted readings

"The danger that cultural analysis, in search of all-too-deep-lying turtles, will lose touch with the hard surfaces of life—with the political, economic, stratificatory realities within which men are everywhere contained—and with the biological and physical necessities on which those surfaces rest, is an ever-present one. The only defense against it, and against, thus, turning cultural analysis into a kind of sociological aestheticism, is to train such analysis on such realities and such necessities in the first place. It is thus that I have written about nationalism, about violence, about identity, about human nature, about legitimacy, about revolution, about ethnicity, about urbanization, about status, about death about time, and most of all about particular attempts by particular peoples to place these things in some sort of comprehensible, meaningful frame."(p.30)

——Geertz, C. (1973). Thick description: Toward an interpretative theory of culture. In *The Interpretation of Cultures*. New York: Basic Books. 3–30.

"The decision to use assessment in this way may not be a conscious one, but it is certainly political, in the sense that it pre-supposes a tacit consensus, a consensus that is constantly reinforced by political decisions and actions. In some education systems, however, the decision-making is highly conscious, and carried out in the name of social cohesion. In circumstances where social cohesion is problematic due to the increasing heterogeneity of a society—a widespread phenomenon in the 21st century due not least to migration—the explicitness of the values is strong and the use of assessment to promote them is more acceptable. Assessment of both *saviors* and *savoirêtre* can thus be deemed desirable."(p.222)

——Byram, M. (2008). *Foreign Language Education to Education for Intercultural Citizenship*. Shanghai: Shanghai Foreign Language Education Press.

"至于说到各种宗教是彼此否认,彼此反对的观念。那是比较宗教哲学上的一个大问题。也可以说,任何一个人,或任何一门学识,因为观点的立场不同,思想推论便完全两样。在我而言,我认为除了所有宗教的形式和教授法之外,任何宗教形而上的精神,都是彼此调和,彼此融通。甚之,可以互相比类注解。因为真理只有一个,正如佛的'不二法门'。禅宗大师们所说的,'除此一事实,余二皆非真'。"(第165页)

——南怀瑾著述.《中国文化泛言》.上海:复旦大学出版社.2016年.

"思想形态古今变易,宗教信仰与物质文明互相抵触,卫道者仅从表面视之,颇为忧

第九节 反思和衡量你的跨文化能力
Theme 9　Reflections and assessments on your IC

愤。殊不知未来科学发展的归趋,正为剖寻昔日宗教的目标,终无二致。过去在民智未开之时,宗教以神秘作风指示生命的真谛。现今以后,科学以精详剖析,寻讨生命神秘之究竟。即俗即真,空有不二,不受形拘,但求神髓,终至两不相妨而相成也。"(第192页)

——南怀瑾著述.《中国文化泛言》.上海:复旦大学出版社.2016年.

"The results of the survey indicate that most of the surveyed Chinese university EFL teachers hold a positive attitude towards ICC assessment, regarding ICC as a necessary part of EFL curriculum and, thus, should be incorporated into foreign language tests. However, the fact that those who actually assessed ICC take up less than half of the total respondents suggests that they still consider linguistic competence as the priority of language assessment, while ICC remains an auxiliary of language learning and is of secondary status. In addition, the respondents' understanding of ICC remains insufficient and even inaccurate. Many equate intercultural teaching with cultural teaching in which culture is treated as a static, fixed body of knowledge of the cultures associated with English-speaking countries. This misguided conception is also reflected in assessment practices where various dimensions of ICC are treated unequally. English culture is perceived to be synonymous with the cultures of mainstream English-speaking countries, while cultures of non-English-speaking countries are ignored."(p.263)

——Gu, X. (2016). Assessment of intercultural communicative competence in FL education: A survey on EFL teachers' perception and practice in China. *Language and Intercultural Communication, 16*, 254–273.

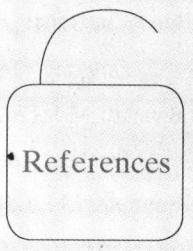

参考文献

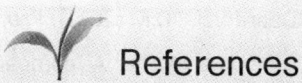
References

Baker, W. (2012). From cultural awareness to intercultural awareness: Culture in ELT. *English Language Teaching*, 66, 62 – 70.

Bennett, M.J. (2013). *Basic Concepts of Intercultural Communication. Paradigms, Principles and Practices.* (*second edition*). Boston & London: Intercultural Press.

Bennett, M.J. (2013). Overcoming the golden rule: Sympathy and empahty. In Bennett. M. J. (Ed.), *Basic Concepts of Intercultural Communication. Paradigms, Principles and Practices* (pp 203 – 233). Boston & London: Intercultural Press.

Borghetti, C. (2017). Is there really a need for assessing intercultural competence? Some ethical issues. *Journal of Intercultural Communication*, 44. http://immi.se/intercultural/nr44/borghetti.html

Byram, M., et al. (2009). *Autobiography of Intercultural Encounters*. https://rm.coe.int/autobiography-of-intercultural-encounters/16806bf02d

Byram, M. (2014). *From Foreign Language Education to Education for Intercultural Citizenship*. Shanghai: Shanghai Foreign Language Education Press.

Bohm, D. (2014). *On Dialogue*. New York: Routledge.

Chen, G. M., & Starosta, W. J. (1998 – 1989). A review of the concept of intercultural awareness. *Human Communication*, 2, 27 – 54.

Deardorff, D. K. (2006). Identification and assessment of intercultural competence as a student outcome of internalization. *Journal of Studies in International Education*, 10(3), 241 – 266.

Deardorff, D.K. (2011). Promoting understanding and development of intercultural dialogue and peace: A comparative analysis and global perspective of regional studies on intercultural competence. *Report of the State of the Arts and Perspectives on Intercultural Competences and Skills*, UNESCO.

Dervin, F. (2017). *Critical Interculturality: Lectures and Notes*. Newcastle: Cambridge Scholars.

Dirlik, A. (1999). Bringing history back in: Of diasporas, hybridities, places, and histories. *Review of Education, Pedagogy, and Cultural Studies*, 21(2), 95 – 131.

Fisher, R., & Ury, W. (2012). *Getting to Yes: Negotiating an Agreement Without Giving In*. London: Random House Business Books.

Geertz, C. (1973). Thick description: Toward an interpretative theory of culture. In *The Interpretation of Cultures*. New York: Basic Books.

Geertz, C. (2012). Thick description: Towards an interpretative theory of culture. In Chen, L. (Ed.), *Culture, Cultures and Intercultural Communication: A Cross Disciplinary Reader*. Shanghai: Shanghai Foreign Language Education Press.

Gudykunst, W.B. (2014, a). An Anxiety/uncertainty management (AUM) theory of effective communication: Making the mesh of the net finer. In Gudykunst, W.B. (Ed.), *Theorizing About Intercultural Communication* (pp. 281–322). Shanghai: Shanghai Foreign Language

Education Press.

Gudykunst, W.B. (2014, b). An Anxiety/uncertainty management (AUM) theory of strangers' intercultural adjustment. In Gudykunst, W. B. (Ed.), *Theorizing About Intercultural Communication* (pp.419 – 457). Shanghai: Shanghai Foreign Language Education Press.

Gu, X. (2016). Assessment of intercultural communicative competence in FL education: A survey on EFL teachers' perception and practice in China. *Language and Intercultural Communication*, 16, 254 – 273.

Hall, S. (1990). Cultural identity and diaspora. In J. Rutherford (Ed.), *Identity: Community, Culture and Difference* (pp.222 – 237). London, UK: Lawrence & Wishart.

Hoffman, E., & Verdooren, A. (2018). *Diversity Competence*. Bussum: Uitgeverij Coutinho.

Holliday, A., Hyde, M., & Kullman, J. (2004). *Intercultural Communication: An Advanced Resource Book for Students*. London & New York: Routledge.

Holliday, A. (2010). Complexity in cultural identity. *Language and Intercultural Communication*, 10(2), 165 – 177.

Holliday, A. (2013). *Understanding Intercultural Communication: Negotiating a Grammar of Culture*. New York: Routledge.

Holliday, A., Kullman, J., & Hyde, M. (2017). *Intercultural Communication: An advanced Resource Book for Students*. Milton Park: Routledge.

Holmes, P., & O'Neill, G. (2012). Developing and evaluating intercultural competence: ethnographies of intercultural encounters. *International Journal of Intercultural Relations*, 36, 707 – 718.

INCA. (2004). Retrieved from: https://ec.europa.eu/migrant-integration/librarydoc/the-inca-project-intercultural-competence-assessment

Jia, Y., et al. (2018). *Experiencing Global Intercultural Communication*. Beijing: Foreign Language Teaching and Research Press.

Jullien, F. (2011). Trans. Richardson, M. & Fijalkowski, K. *The Silent Transformations*. Calcutta: Seagull Books.

Kim, M. S. (2014). Cultural-based conversational constraints theory: Individual- and cultural-level analyses. In Gudykunst W. B. (Ed.), *Theorizing About Intercultural Communication*. Shanghai: Shanghai Foreign Language Education Press.

Kramsch, C. (1998). *Language and Culture*. Oxford: Oxford University Press.

Kohls, L. R. (2009). Why do Americans act like that? In Zhuang, E., & Kalstein, H. (Eds.), *English Reading Course for Intercultural Perspectives* 3 (pp.34 – 38). Shanghai: Shanghai Foreign Language Education Press.

Kulich, S.J. (2010). Toward an integrated identity matrix theory(IIMT)—Proposals for a dynamic cultural identity framework. In Dai, X., & Kulich, S. J. (Eds.), *Identity and Intercultural Communication (I): Theoretical and Contextual Construction* (pp.69 – 102).

Shanghai: Shanghai Foreign Language Education Press.

Liu, Y. (2015). *East Meets West*. Krohne: Taschen.

Mills, C. W. (2016). *The Sociological Imagination*. Beijing: Press of Communication University of China.

Rickles, D. (2014). Foreword to the Routledge Great Minds Edition. In Bohm, D. *On Dialogue*. New York: Routledge.

Spencer-Oatey, H., & Franklin, P. (2010). *Intercultural Interaction: A Multidisciplinary Approach to Intercultural Communication*. Shanghai: Foreign Language Teaching and Research Press.

Starosta, W. J. (2010). Expanding the circumference of centrisms: On the reframing of identity. In Dai, X., & Kulich, S. J. (Eds.), *Identity and Intercultural Communication (I): Theoretical and Contextual Construction* (pp. 53 – 68). Shanghai: Shanghai Foreign Language Education Press.

Tarde, G. (2016). *Communication and Social Influence*. Beijing: Chinese Communication University Press.

Ting-Toomey, S. (2007). *Communicating Across Cultures*. Shanghai: Shanghai Foreign Language Education Press.

Van Maele J., & Mertens, K. (2014). Towards an experience-driven approach to teaching intercultural communication. In: Romanowski, P. (Ed.), *Studia Naukowe, 27, Intercultural issues in the era of globalization* (pp.122–129). Warsaw: IKSI Scientific Publishing House.

Van Maele, J., Vassilicos, B., & Borghetti, C. (2016). Mobile students' appraisals of keys to a successful stay aboard experience: Hints from the IEREST project. *Language and Intercultural Communication*, 3, 384–401.

Yu, Q. & Van Maele, J. (2018). Fostering intercultural awareness in a Chinese English reading class. *Chinese Journal of Applied Linguistics*, 3, 357–275.

白利鹏. 生活世界：非本质主义的总体性如何可能[J]. 社会科学研究，2008,(6)：6-11.

贝内特,米尔顿·J. 超越黄金法则：同情与移情. 米尔顿·J. 贝内特编著. 跨文化交流的建构与实践[M]. 关世杰,何惺译. 北京：北京大学出版社，2012.

贝内特,米尔顿·J. 跨文化交流的建构与实践[M]. 关世杰,何惺译. 北京：北京大学出版社，2012.

戴晓东. 解读跨文化认同的四种视角[J]. 学术研究，2013,(9)：144-151.

德里达,雅克. 解构与思想的未来[M]. 夏可君编校. 吉林：吉林人民出版社，2006.

德里克,阿里夫. 历史回归：关于离散、混杂、地点和历史. 何成洲编. 跨学科视野下的文化身份认同[C]. 北京：北京大学出版社，2011.

董健. 全球化与文化民族主义. 何成洲编. 跨学科视野下的文化身份认同[C]. 北京：北

京大学出版社，2011.

樊东译注. 尚书[M]. 上海：三联书店，2013.

冯海颖，黄大网. 跨文化交际研究：从本质主义到批判现实主义[J]. 外语界，2016，(1)：61-69.

甘小亚，黄莹雪，程桑桑. 多模态的跨文化交际能力测评模式[J]. 沈阳工业大学学报（社会科学版），2018，(1)：92-96.

亨廷顿，塞缪尔. 文明的冲突[M]. 周琪等译. 北京：新华出版社，2012.

黄寿祺，周善文. 周易译注[M]. 系辞上传. 第九章. 上海：上海古籍出版社. 2010.

霍尔，爱德华. 超越文化[M]. 中译本第二版序. 何道宽译. 北京：北京大学出版社，2011.

吉噶·康楚仁波切. 无我的智慧[M]. 丁乃竺译. 西安：陕西师范大学出版总社有限公司，2010.

乐黛云. 跨越文化边界[M]. 上海：东方出版中心，2012.

李少龙. 中国传统文化中的"难得糊涂"思想[J]. 南开学报（哲学社会科学版），2005，(6)：70-79.

列维纳斯，伊曼纽尔. 总体与无限：论外在性[M]. 朱刚译. 北京：北京大学出版社，2016.

卢森堡，马歇尔. 非暴力沟通[M]. 阮胤华译. 北京：华夏出版社，2018.

南怀瑾. 中国文化泛言[M]. 上海：复旦大学出版社，2016.

汪子嵩. 希腊哲学史：1卷[M]. 北京：人民文学出版社，1997.

王明珂. 反思性研究与当代中国民族认同[J]. 南京大学学报（哲学人文科学社会科学版），2008，(1)：55-67.

吴建生. 泉州讲古新编[C]. 福州：福建人民出版社，2008.

吴图南讲授. 马有清编著. 太极拳之研究——吴图南太极功[M]. 香港：世纪图书出版公司，后浪出版公司，2013-2014.

吴莹. 文化、群体与认同：社会心理学的视角[M]. 北京：社会科学文献出版社，2016.

杨述伊. 跨文化教学中的测试体系研究[J]. 吉林师范大学学报（人文社会科学版），2013，(1)：105-108.

张迎忠. 谈太极拳松功的作用与训练[J]. 搏击，2007，(12)：61-62.

张志明. 太极拳放松的理论体系[J]. 中华武术，2017，(5)：64-67.

周宪. 换种方式说"艺术边界"[J]. 北京大学学报（哲学社会科学版），2016，(6)：19-26.

祝大彤. 太极无处不放松[J]. 精武，2005，(10)：42.

祝大彤. 触人如放电——太极拳的松功[J]. 精武，2005，(11)：31.

图书在版编目(CIP)数据

跨文化能力:学习与实训/于群编著.—南京:
南京大学出版社,2020.9
ISBN 978-7-305-23490-3

Ⅰ.①跨… Ⅱ.①于… Ⅲ.①文化交流-研究 Ⅳ.
①G115

中国版本图书馆 CIP 数据核字(2020)第 109921 号

出版发行 南京大学出版社
社　　址 南京市汉口路22号　　邮编　210093
出 版 人 金鑫荣

书　　名 跨文化能力:学习与实训
编　　著 于 群
责任编辑 刁晓静

照　　排 南京开卷文化传媒有限公司
印　　刷 南京人民印刷厂有限责任公司
开　　本 787×1092　1/16　印张 12.5　字数 274 千
版　　次 2020 年 9 月第 1 版　2020 年 9 月第 1 次印刷
ISBN 978-7-305-23490-3
定　　价 39.80 元

网　　址:http://www.njupco.com
官方微博:http://weibo.com/njupco
微信服务号:njuyuexue
销售咨询热线:(025)83594756

* 版权所有,侵权必究
* 凡购买南大版图书,如有印装质量问题,请与所购
　图书销售部门联系调换